FEAR AND LOATHING IN DUBLIN

AODHAN MADDEN

LIB
ERT
IES

1

The day's shift on the *Evening Press* was over and, as usual, some of the sub-editors sought solace in the grimy back lounge of Mulligan's in Poolbeg Street. We were watching Bernadette Devlin making a speech in New York. 'Up the IRA!' someone shouted, and there was a general murmur of approval. I was drinking with Adrian McLoughlin, the acerbic film critic of the *Evening Press*. He rarely saw any of the films he was supposed to have reviewed but that did not detract from the entertainment value of his Saturday column. His film pieces were wild, intoxicated essays. He said that he was thirty-six but he looked more than fifty. He was small and tubby and his clothes were a riot of colours; he bought them in a boutique called 'Hot Pants' off Henry Street in the centre of Dublin. This afternoon he was wearing pink, skintight trousers, over which his beer belly flopped like a gigantic codpiece. He was painfully conscious of his retreating hairline and was forever cultivating the last bits of straggly vegetation. I often saw him combing his hair on the street, one eye furtively scrutinising his reflection in a shop window.

'Fuck Bernadette Devlin!' Adrian roared at the television set. This elicited a murmur of approval from some of the newspapermen in the bar. Tom, the barman, looked affronted. He was young and from the country, and was very sensitive to any disparagement of his republican beliefs. 'Now, Adrian, keep it down,' he warned, his fat, rubbery face flushed with indignation.

But Adrian wanted to talk about the book he was writing and the strident Northern platitudes emanating from the television disrupted his flow because she was adored by the entire country. He hated the common cause and relished being aloof from anything that was fashionable.

We went to Mulligan's every afternoon. Sometimes the newspaper's editor, Conor Byrne, joined us for a gin and tonic, but he rarely talked and liked to stand slightly apart. Adrian believed that Conor, who was from Blackrock, was a snob. Certainly Conor exuded a certain gravitas, as if the responsibilities of being an editor of a Dublin evening newspaper had elevated him above the rest of us. He talked about rugby, and his friends were mostly barristers and judges – rather seedy-looking, turkey-wattled gentlemen who dropped in to Mulligan's on their way home from the courts.

'Adrian, let's talk about something else apart from your fucking book.' I was bored by his obsessive retelling of every verse and chapter of his magnum opus. His face clouded over and his eyes narrowed viciously behind the broken glasses – the result of one of his 'falls' when he was going home at night from the pub.

'Let's talk about you, ye mean,' he hissed. 'Let's talk about you and your fucking trendy friends up in the Bailey.'

There was jealous rage in his voice. He was consumed

with bitterness. Most of the time this anger was chan-
nelled into drunken eccentricity, but when it became personal, it was very disturbing. Why did he hate me so
much? Yet he followed me around everywhere. He even
tried to dress like me, desperately attempting to be the
twenty-year-old that I was then in 1971 and that he apparently had never been. The Bailey, to him, was the
repository of everything that was crass, modern and fashionable. It was 'up there', off Grafton Street, where the
new generation strutted and pouted like peacocks, and
was a world away from Adrian's decrepit old Dublin of
newspaper 'characters' and Georgian ghosts.

Mick Barlow, an irascible court reporter, sidled into
our company, attracted by the prospect of trouble. Barlow
was tiny and wizened; he wore a floral bow tie and sported
a malevolent gargoyle grin. He had spent too many years
in the courts, reporting on murders and rapes and the
seamy side of human experience. His jaded manner
hinted at long afternoons at dismal press receptions, sipping cheap wine and munching wet cheese crackers with
flashy types in mohair suits.

'Ah, Adrian,' he said, 'I hear you are about to take the
literary world by storm.' A smirk cracked his face.

This remark did the trick, and Adrian was stopped in
full flow of invective.

Barlow winked at me mischievously. 'And may one enquire what the manuscript is called?' he asked in a
mocking tone.

Adrian snorted and drained the last of his pint.
'Footsteps in the Scullery,' he said sharply.

Barlow's eyes rose in mock appreciation. 'How

suggestive of a lower-middle-class Joycean mileu. It is set in Dublin, I presume?'

Of course, this had the desired effect, and Adrian was off again, bustling through the maze of the book's plot. Barlow's eyes now suddenly glittered and his mock wistful sighs encouraged Adrian in his hopeless, useless, drunken odyssey.

I turned back to the television. At least Bernadette Devlin had honesty and passion going for her. She was not like these cynics in Mulligan's. They were running a national newspaper, yet they were so bored, so weighed down by their own hopelessness, that they could not believe in anything any more, not even themselves. The pub filled up with more reporters and printers. The winter afternoon darkened and I got drunk again.

The subs desk in the *Press* was like a home for terminal eccentrics. They were mostly middle-aged men in varying stages of mental and physical disrepair. Some had stopped talking to others years before. Others were so permanently drunk and wet-brained that they merely went through the motions of editing copy. Readers who rang in to complain about misprints in the paper had no inkling of the bedlam behind the typographical chaos. The cause of much of this anarchy was Harry O'Toole, a former priest who wore a green gansey that looked like a Picasso painting with the egg and soup stains of a lifetime gathered in it. He was the sub who had spiked a breaking news report about the Six Day War because he'd had to catch the four o'clock bus home to Bray, where he kept a guest house. No mere war was going to interfere with his domestic arrangements.

Then there was John J. Dunne, who, apart from his sub-editing duties, wrote ghost stories for the paper. He was obsessed with ghosts and murders and knew more about Dr Crippen and Jack the Ripper than he ever did about journalism. A bachelor in his sixties, he was so insecure that he had to possess two of everything: two houses, two cars, two dogs, and apparently only two shirts. His insecurity made him ferociously intense. I once sold him a pair of elephant flares for two pounds. He proudly wore them around the office. Adrian said that he looked like a scarecrow; but a bargain, even one that might make an ageing man look vaguely ridiculous, was still a bargain. His home-made 'fry sandwiches' were an office joke. At eleven every morning, he produced this oddity from his satchel – two ugly lumps of bread clamped over a fried egg, black pudding and a tomato – and fed upon it with the fury of a barracuda.

For a few years, I revelled in this strange, witty world of middle-aged male eccentricity. But it was also a selfish and cruel world. The laughter was harsh – like that of hyenas feasting on the marrow of human frailty. There was a lot of fear, too: a sense of impending doom. At around seven in the evening, after spending three hours or more in Mulligan's, I used to get the number 10 bus home to the North Circular Road. I was usually inebriated, and my mother was often angry. 'You'll ruin your life,' she used to say, fearfully.

I knew she was right, but what other life was there apart from Mulligan's and the Bailey and occasionally

Searson's over in Baggot Street? Life was in the pubs and the clubs, in the back room of Groome's Hotel in Parnell Square, where what passed for the Dublin *demi-monde* assembled after the pubs had closed. I was young and this was a young age. The economic depression was over and we had money in our pockets for the first time. Besides, I was writing a column in the *Sunday Press* and I was often on the radio reviewing plays. What other twenty-year-old was doing these things? I had it made, I kept telling myself. Even if I woke up in a gutter of vomit and blood in one of the lanes at the back of the *Press*, I knew I had it made. I often stumbled home to hammer out some smart-ass review on the typewriter and impress the world. Oh yes, I impressed the world all right.

Bernadette Devlin might have been loathed by many of the older generation, but to us younger people she was a heroine, the voice of persecuted Irish nationalism. She linked us to the great youth protests of the age, to Alexander Dubcek in Prague, the students at the barricades in Paris, the anti-Vietnam war protesters outside American embassies around the world. I knew very little about Northern Ireland, though. Some of my grandmother's people had been burned out of Belfast in the 1920s, but the Orangemen were stranger to me than aliens from a distant planet.

After Bloody Sunday, when the SAS shot down thirteen unarmed civilians in Derry, the country went mad. Adrian and I joined the mob outside the British Embassy in Merrion Square. We were both mouldy drunk – as were, it seemed, most people, walking around in the drizzle that winter's day like extras in a ghastly melodrama. Every time one of the Sinn Féiners lobbed a petrol bomb from their lorry up at the embassy, a drunken cheer went up. 'Go home, ye fuckin' Black and Tans!' a boy, aged about ten, screamed up at the beautiful Georgian building. I noticed a neighbour of mine on the back of the Sinn Féin lorry. He was generally a quiet, simple man but had now suddenly been transformed into a salivating lunatic, as he urged us all to storm the building. We had absolutely no doubt that right was on our side: there was no space in that frantic place for the merest hint of doubt.

When it was all over, we trudged back through the January gloom to the solace of Mulligan's, elated because we had done our bit for Ireland. The atmosphere in the pub was electric, like that after an All-Ireland football final. There is nowhere quite like a newspaper pub when a big story breaks: it is all as phoney as the Hollywood stereotype, with reporters pumped up on self-importance and piddling about like children playing Shakespeare. Clichés became the poetry of anguished inarticulation. Great emotions were described in garish brushstrokes, and a moment of great historical importance was reduced to a facile headline.

Not long after that, Dublin was hit by a series of bomb scares; the *Irish Press* was an obvious target for loyalist terrorists. Every time there was a scare, we evacuated the old building to seek refuge in one of the pubs on Burgh Quay beside the Liffey. The Scotch House was like an old barn. It attracted a strange mix of newspaper people, actors and, sometimes, rent boys, who cruised the quay in search of customers. One Saturday afternoon during a bomb scare, I was sitting at the bar observing a

High Court judge making eyes at a scruffy young male customer of about eighteen when Adrian stumbled in sport-
ing a black eye and looking as if he had fallen out of an old
painting.

'I was beaten up by a priest,' he said. He refused to
elaborate and I knew from experience that it was point-
less to pursue the matter. Adrian was not just a drunk, he
was a free spirit, and that was what had brought me into
his crazy orbit. He lived his life in pubs and knew the secrets of all their inhabitants, but he could never write anything more substantial than the journalism pieces that he
tossed off for the newspaper. There were books in him
all right – a whole library of bibulous tales which would
never be written down but would instead be acted out to
strangers in pubs. I sensed that he knew that he was
trapped in this literary twilight. He told the world that he
was writing his great book, but nobody believed him.

Later, I learned that he had been beaten up by two cler-
ics in the grounds of Clonliffe College, Drumcondra, after
they had been awakened by his drunken bawling: 'Fuck
the archbishop! Fuck the archbishop!' The archbishop in
question was the legendary John Charles McQuaid, with
whom Adrian was obsessed. He hated the old autocrat and
regularly regaled his pub cronies with outrageous stories
concerning McQuaid's alleged sexual practices.

Adrian nodded to the High Court judge and then, to
my amazement, ordered a pint of lemonade. 'I'm giving up
the drink,' he solemnly declared. Of course I didn't believe him. 'I can't drink and write at the same time,' he said.
'So now I have to rewrite the book again.' I had thought
that the sudden crisis in the North had pushed that

particular obsession out of his mind. But no, it was still there, gnawing at him, a ghastly mammoth defying extinction. Then he gave me a strange, unsettling look. 'I have to write it, you see.' So he returned to his typewriter and rewrote many thousands more words of petrified prose which no publisher would ever read. He must have read my mind, because he slammed his pint glass onto the counter. 'I'll show you, you little fucking bastard.' Downwind, the judge knocked back his glass of whiskey and loped wearily back into the jungle.

Terry O'Sullivan wrote a social column in the paper every evening. His 'Dubliners' Diary' archly described a Dublin that was still cosily provincial. But now, in the early 1970s, that was changing. The old shabby city was disappearing as new office blocks replaced the music halls, cinemas and run-down Georgian buildings. The old-style newspaper columnist, who came into the office in evening dress reeking of whiskey and eau de cologne, was beginning to look like a pomaded extra from another age.

One evening, O'Sullivan mentioned to me that the American singer Guy Mitchell was making a comeback in, of all places, the Drake Inn, a somewhat tacky pub out in Finglas. He gave me one of his extravagant matinée winks. 'That's up your alley, old chum,' he said, referring to a recent series of articles I had done for the paper called 'Where are they now?' This was an exercise in journalistic necrophilia which involved raiding hospitals, nursing homes and drying-out clinics in pursuit of actors, politicians and sports stars of yore – the flotsam of a vanished celebrity circuit. One such 'celebrity' was a former Theatre Royal matinée idol, Freddy Doyle, now ancient, rouged and sitting on a bed in Baggot Street Hospital surrounded by yellowed newspaper cuttings. He went on and on about the Boer War, and after a while I realised that he regarded me as a contemporary.

'Ye must remember Madge Cliften,' he said. 'She shot her lover in the arse and went off to South America, where she died in the war.'

'Which war, Freddy?'

'The Boer War,' he rasped.

The Drake Inn was crammed with middle-aged ladies. As soon as Guy Mitchell limped arthritically on to the tiny stage, a great raucous roar went up from the peroxide ranks. He sang his trademark song 'She Wore Red Feathers on her Hoola-hoola Skirt', and the grannies of Finglas sang along adoringly. Then Guy plunged into all his other hits of the 1950s, stopping occasionally to sip from a pint of Guinness. The voice was gone and he looked haggard. It was sad, yet his fans were in a celebratory mood. Here was their great childhood hero returned – ravaged and shell-shocked, but alive – from the wars. Afterwards, in a Corporation house beside the pub, I chatted to Mitchell about his comeback. 'Yeah,' he announced with the doomed enthusiasm of a loser, he was going on to London and then Las Vegas. We never heard of him after that.

Not long after that scoop, I was back on the necrophile trail again. For some reason, the paper's editor thought I was best employed trudging down memory lane. It was safer there for a young drunk.

Kathleen Behan, Brendan's mother, was celebrating her

birthday in her nursing home in Raheny. It was a bright, cheerful Friday afternoon, but the ward was as tranquil as a convent, with elderly patients snoozing behind their bed-screens. The sun, bursting in the windows, cast a remorseless light on this Limbo, but Kathleen was in high spirits. She asked me to stand guard at the ward door while she smoked a cigarette. 'The Mother Superior will kill me,' she chuckled.

We talked for hours about her life in Russell Street, with her unruly brood of brilliantly talented children; about Brendan, and his adventures, and his tragically early death. She described a past teeming with life, humour and tragedy. A deep sadness hung over us; I thought about what a lonely last act to such a riotously rich life this was.

'You'll visit me again,' she whispered as I left her. 'I don't get too many visitors now.'

Kathleen died a few weeks later.

Occasionally I did theatre reviews for the *Evening Press*. Once I reviewed a play called *When Did You Last See Your Mother?* by Christopher Hampton. The play was about a young man's painful attempts to come to terms with his homosexuality. In my review, I appealed for a more compassionate attitude to gay people. A few days after the review was published, a priest from our parish called to the house to 'have a word' with me. He said he was 'most concerned' about the views I had expressed in the paper. I brusquely told him that he should write a letter to the editor, who might consider publishing it, and then showed him to the door. The incident disturbed me, though, and

I decided to keep certain views to myself.

It was safer to trawl down memory lane. I had found my perfect niche in this kind of journalism. The past had always been a favourite place of refuge for me. It was everywhere, beckoning from family photographs, from old newspapers under the linoleum in my bedroom, from every dusty nook and cranny of our Victorian house on the North Circular Road. And the past was like a drug, a soothing soporific. Belonging to a large extended family meant being part of living history. Pop talked about the Troubles with old cronies from the neighbourhood, recalling with relish the derring-do of IRA men on the run from the British forces. He also talked about the bravery of the Dublin Fusiliers in the Great War. Mother remembered how her Uncle Terry, a mere boy, had been dragged from his bed and beaten up by the Black and Tans. And there were the aunts, or 'the girls', as Mother called them. They were Pop's three unmarried sisters, who lived together on the Cabra Road and idolised the only man in their lives – Éamon de Valera. They inhabited the past completely: all their energies were drawn from it. Their talk was about childhood holidays in an enchanted Greystones; the Eucharistic Congress and Count John McCormack singing 'Panis Angelicus'; de Valera's wartime tussles with Churchill; Monday nights spent swooning at camp English music-hall artistes in the Theatre Royal. Even when they came for the Christmas parties, they brought the past with them. They drank sherry and sang Edwardian-era songs, and Anna, the eldest and most accomplished of the three, played Ivor Novello tunes on the piano.

From an early age, I was convinced that the past was an ideal place. All the best music belonged there. So too did the happiest times: of sunlit summer days and fire-warmed winter nights when that exquisite music of remembrance wafted up the stairs to my room, and maiden aunts sang about love and regret. It was impossible to resist the pull of the past when, as a child, I viewed the future with nervous uncertainty. And of course, the past was the safest refuge for a drunk. Even the subs desk in the *Press* resembled a world closer to that of James Joyce than to the changing Ireland of the 1970s. It was peopled by 'characters' – Dublin shorthand for mild eccentrics, perverts, bigots, manic depressives, hopeless alcoholics and raving lunatics. And the nearby pubs belonged to a pre-1914 world. They were dirty and musty, their walls yellowed by years of cigarette smoke, their snugs and back rooms inhabited by gnarled and crabbed creatures redolent of Hogarth – creatures who were also besotted with the past, the 1930s or 1940s, when newspapers were supposedly better and reporters were fearless champions of the truth. And on weekend nights, these pubs were like Babels of ancient chaos, as the old crowd recycled all their fantasies with maudlin gusto.

Of course, the past fertilised and stimulated our politics as well: the North, England, the Famine and 1916. We thought we were hip, in our elephant flares and platform boots, but we were still rooted in some backwater of history, endlessly singing the same sentimental airs, furiously mouthing the anti-English lyrics of the Wolfe Tones in grubby ballad bars. We might have protested against the Vietnam war outside the American Embassy, but only imperial Britain could inspire our deepest feelings of self-pity and racial hatred. We turned up at the anti-apartheid rallies, but no issue was ever as serious, as personal and as emotional as the 'eight hundred years' of England's so-called colonial tyranny.

Adrian and John J. Dunne seemed to typify that age for me. I wanted to be like them – brilliant writers who were focused entirely on old Dublin, unsolved murders, ghost stories, the personal and anecdotal details of battles long ago. All their energies came, it seemed, from that miasma, and I was, for a while, dazzled. I walked O'Connell Street and saw only ghosts: an impossibly romantic Robert Emmet or Patrick Pearse, with their mad eyes and good looks; Parnell and Kitty O'Shea and the battalions of jealous priests; Maud Gonne swooping on a public rally outside the Rotunda like an ancient bird of prey; Micheál MacLiammóir swanning into the Gresham Hotel in hideous make-up like a Byzantine emperor. MacLiammóir was Dublin's token gay celebrity. Most people thought that he and his partner, Hilton Edwards, were the only gay people in Ireland; they were tolerated because of MacLiammóir's status as a great 'Irish' actor.

Dublin's idealised past was heady wine indeed, and I drank on it to stupefaction. I drank from the very first day I joined the *Press* after leaving school at eighteen. Drink was to be the great liberation from a 1950s Irish childhood. It was to be a grand adventure, opening up all the secrets of the forbidden. 'You'll ruin yourself,' Mother warned, but I never heeded her. I used to see that fearful look in her eyes when I stumbled in drunk after a night in Mulligan's and the back room of Groome's Hotel. That look came from the past, from a country town where an uncle had drunk himself into an early grave, and where many boys and girls my own age had sunk into a similar mire of booze and mawkishness. History was working its malevolent spell on another generation, she must have felt, and she was helpless to stop it.

'I wish you had never gone into the *Press*,' she said another time. Her disappointment was all the more painful because she could never understand or articulate it. The simple girl from Tipperary was proud of the achievements of her children, but beneath that pride there was a deep, dull, inexplicable ache that no amount of bylines and interviews with the famous could remove. I think she must have glimpsed my future, but she was not to live to see her deepest fears realised.

2

Mother fell out of the bath one morning. I remember that the radio was on, crackling with furious Northern voices. It was 9 August 1971, the day they introduced internment in Northern Ireland. My sister called the doctor but he never came. Then, in panic, we called an ambulance and Mother was taken to the Mater Hospital, where they discovered that she had suffered a minor heart attack. She rallied for a few days and her personality filled the ward. She seemed to know all the other patients – where they came from, their relations and friends. Mother was always saying in wonderment: 'Isn't it a small world all the same?' After about a week, she had recovered sufficiently, and the doctors said she could return home within a day or two.

Then the phone rang at 6 AM one Monday morning. I heard it and ran down the stairs, but Pop had already taken the call. He said gravely that we were to go down to the hospital. But I knew what he knew and resented that even then, at this critical hour, he was trying to shield us from the truth. At the hospital, I noticed nurses rushing in and out of the ward. Other nurses were removing a drip from Mother's bed, which had a screen around it. Then I saw Pop bent over in pain. There was a suddenness about everything which was appalling: the terrible drip, the white figures darting about, the spontaneous gasps, and the jerky movements of shock. It all felt like a dream. I can recall walking in what seemed to me to be slow motion, in that white, dreamlike chaos.

The next few days passed in a daze. People were coming and going to the house. There was a heightened sense of movement, of people murmuring and then dashing off. There was no room for the enormity of it all to sink in. That was to take place gradually over the next months and years, when we tried to accustom ourselves to a house that had been robbed of its leading spirit. Pop kept working for a while, but he suddenly became an old man. I could hear him crying in his room late at night. This was his private grief, which he could not share with us. Security died with my mother. One day, we had belonged to a family and a household that revolved around her; the next day, that centre was gone and we drifted aimlessly into our own selves.

When they brought me to see her laid out in the mortuary, my abiding impression was that she was not my mother at all. She had shrunk into an ancient cadaver, bereft of that spirit which had been the source of all our lives. This was not the beautiful, brown-eyed country girl of my parents' wedding photo. I had to look away. I could only keep her in my memory now, but all too soon even memory proved no guarantor of intimacy. Her spirit faded from the house, and from our lives. Over the years, she receded back in time, to the point where even her face became difficult to recall.

I walked out of the hospital that Monday morning and

into the warren of little streets off Berkeley Road. I should have stayed to comfort my father, but I wanted to drift with my thoughts through these humble side streets, with their neatly painted houses. I needed to refresh myself with the familiar and the commonplace, to gaze at ordinary things: garden gnomes, flower boxes on windowsills, frilly curtains, a woman polishing her brass doorknob. Already, guilt was beginning to gnaw away at me. My mother worried about me so much: about my drinking; about my not having a bank account, or a car, or a girlfriend; about my not fitting in to the normal patterns. I was to shed many tears for the loss of her in the years after, when I began to realise that I had let her go out of my life without the merest struggle. That knowledge could be endured only with the aid of alcohol. I had no idea what the shape of the future might be.

Walking around Berkeley Road, I sensed that there would be great change, but all my energy was directed towards the familiar. The past was familiar. I sought it out as a means of escape from pain and confusion. I remembered a bowl of jelly on the kitchen table, and sticking my finger in it. A stranger had scolded me. I didn't know who she was. She was a big woman with a red face, dressed all in blue. I ran up through the house until I came to a room, and there was Mother in bed with another stranger, a baby. I asked Mother if I was being sent away with the strange woman, and she beckoned me, with a reassuring laugh, into her bed.

I remembered a Christmas night. My two brothers and I were in bed pretending to be asleep, but really anticipating Santa's arrival. I sneaked down the stairs to make sure that Santa hadn't already come. I heard murmuring in the drawing room. I tiptoed in. The lights on the Christmas tree cast red shadows across the walls. She and Pop were sitting on the couch, holding hands. I watched them for a moment, then slipped back up the stairs again to sleep the soundest sleep of childhood.

The changes wrought by her death were immediate and traumatic. I began to drink heavily and to come home drunk more often. The pub was a refuge from grief as much as from an empty house. There was only myself and Pop: my brothers and sisters had married and moved away. The house became gradually quieter. The biggest change was in Pop himself. He came into his own in the months and years after Mother died. He developed domestic skills: cooking, cleaning, washing up, doing the things which I had never seen him do before. He gradually gave up his building-contracting work until a day came when he no longer donned his overalls. His customers, who were mostly elderly women from the locality, called about their burst pipes and leaking roofs, but it was to no avail: he had finished with work altogether. He sold his car, applied for the old-age pension, and slowly took over my mother's role as housekeeper, to a diminished family. He mapped out his day accordingly: up at ten to his customary breakfast of black pudding, rashers, six slices of bread and cups of tea as strong as tar. Then he went to the supermarket to buy whatever groceries were needed. Thrift being second nature to men of his generation, his shopping basket contained the cheapest foods he could find. His afternoon was spent making the dinner. Irish stews were his speciality, but they often contained lumps of tobacco, which he would have inadvertently let drop into the pot. Then, after dinner, he cleaned himself up, put on his good clothes and walked down to the six o'-clock Mass in Aughrim Street.

His thriftiness led to eccentricity. He recycled everything, from old clothes to used teabags, and tea towels and J-cloths, long discarded, found their way back again into the domestic system. Once I met him coming from Mass and he seemed to have grown a foot taller. Then I saw the reason for his startling change in stature: he was wearing a pair of hideous 1970s platform-heeled boots which I had thrown out years earlier.

Pop had left school at fourteen after my grandfather's sudden death. He spent the rest of his life trying to compensate for that abrupt end to his schooling. He read everything, from Dickens to Agatha Christie, and prided himself on his ability to recite chunks of Goldsmith's 'The Deserted Village', usually pausing to reflect ironically on the line 'How one small head could carry all it knew.' His politics were Labour. He admired Noel Browne and hated de Valera.

Gradually, we became very close. The house itself was actually falling down around us. Pop was getting too old to continue patching it up, and I was usually drinking too much to notice the loose slates, faulty wiring and creaking floorboards. When the damp began to seep through the back wall, he came up with a novel solution: he draped old coats behind the ivy to soak up the moisture. Of course, in time the ivy withered away, to reveal his bizarre artwork.

He possessed a dry sense of humour, which complemented his eccentric ways. Once, Adrian McLoughlin rang in great distress, pretending to be his brother. 'Adrian has passed away,' he said. Pop sympathised with the bereaved 'brother' and said what a wonderful guy Adrian had been and how the world would miss him. When I came home later that night, Pop called out from his bedroom: 'Your friend Adrian rang to say he was dead.'

He had great compassion for people and possessed an acute and kindly insight into human nature. My stories about the strange goings-on in the *Press* never surprised him. Last thing at night, he used to walk around the house, checking every room and locking doors and windows. There were a few holy pictures hanging on the walls – the Sacred Heart, Christ with His crown of thorns (which terrified us as children), and the Virgin – and these he touched every night in silent prayer. Finally, he retired to his room, where he sucked Glacier mints until sleep came.

He often talked about hearing the laughter of ghostly children in the house. I suspect that as he got older, he wandered back into his own past more and more. He certainly talked more about his mother and father in those years; when he did, he was no longer a man in his seventies but a child, still in awe of his parents.

I often tried to tease his secrets out of him when we sat by the fire in the basement living room on winter evenings. Sometimes I felt that I was getting close, but he usually evaded the question or clammed up, puffing on his pipe and gazing thoughtfully into the flames. Even in his final illness, he could not really tell me what had gone wrong. 'I'm all right,' he assured me as he wearily came down the stairs, looking weak, old and changed. He wanted to protect me from reality, *his* reality, and sometimes I wanted to shake him until the truth rattled out of him.

In the years after Mother died, his great mission was to look after me. I had some kind of demon in my head. 'He'll pull out of it,' he said when my brothers and sisters, friends, employers, and even the doctors, had consigned me to the scrapheap. He distrusted doctors and hospitals, and reckoned that the only way that I could ever get better was through gentle support and a peaceful home life. But he could not see that his fatherly loyalty was also complicating the problem. For years during my twenties, I felt trapped in an old man's rhythm, incapable of communicating my own fears and anxieties. He made my meals, cleaned up after me, visited me in hospital and tore up the suicide notes I had hidden about the house. And he never complained. He was doing his duty. Then, when the pressure built up to boiling point and self-pity drove me into some gargantuan binges, he waited patiently for the storm to pass over. He would come to St Patrick's Hospital with clean clothes and toiletries, sit beside my bed in the ward and talk to me as if we were sitting at home beside the fire. He must have been hurt and baffled by it all. He must also have despaired of me sometimes, but he never showed it. He maintained a quiet show of ordinariness even in the most extraordinary situations.

3

The summer of 1976 was balmy. For weeks, the sun burned relentlessly and Dublin began to look like a dusty southern European city. The sun reached places that rarely saw daylight: the damp and dreary corners of pubs, the gloomy back kitchens of the Victorian houses on the North Circular Road. It also lit up people's lives, exposing a city suddenly stirring itself after decades of depression. Young people strode about cheerfully in their floral shirts, humming Abba tunes and enjoying the freedoms that come from having clear skies and money in your pocket. Love was in the air, and we believed the illusion.

Women were asserting their rights in the media and in the workplace. In that blazing summer, it seemed that Ireland had at last thrown off her black clerical weeds and had glimpsed a golden secular future. Sex was no longer taboo. Contraception and divorce were discussed on the airwaves. The bishops objected, but the harm had gone out of their clout. Girls strolled down Grafton Street in the skimpiest of miniskirts, and if bishops blushed, they did so in the isolation of their palaces – so unlike twenty years before, when Archbishop John Charles McQuaid had issued a Pastoral condemning the practice of women cycling around the city in breezy weather, lest their exposed legs give cause for scandal or 'bad thoughts'.

The People's Gardens in the Phoenix Park never looked so beautiful as in that gloriously short-lived summer. Red roses danced and dazzled like cancan girls in the bright sunlight. I often went there in the afternoons after finishing work in the *Press*. Sometimes I pub-crawled my way from Mulligan's to the Ormond Hotel to the Brazen Head, and then on to Ryan's of Parkgate Street. And I would sit in the sun in a drunken stupor, giddy in the knowledge that the Enlightenment had caught up with us at last.

The Phoenix Park was really our back garden. It was a mere hundred or so yards away from home, and so we grew up listening to the roars of lions and the chattering of monkeys in the zoo. The Park also exerted a strange fascination over me: there was something dark and forbidden behind its beautiful exterior. Once, when I was twelve, I walked up there one summer's evening and caught a glimpse of a world of predatory sexuality which was as unsettling as it was dangerously exciting. Here, in what I thought of as my back garden, were strange creatures loitering and beckoning. I sat on the steps of the Wellington Monument and watched the shadows darting about. I saw the cars cruise along the road, stop, pick up their cargo and vanish again into the night. I was fascinated. Yet those images had haunted me in my teenage years. I would lie in bed at night listening for the sounds of the jungle. Did I wander up there as a child of about six or seven? In a recurring dream, my head is being pressed into the wet soil. I am choking; my nostrils are clogged up with clay. Someone is on top of me, moaning, pulling my hair. The next moment in the dream I am looking through the railings of the zoo at the elephants. A mound of elephant dung is steaming nearby. A man, wearing a uniform, takes a bundle of coins from his pocket and lets me pick one. The dream was so horrible, I never dared examine it. Yet whenever I went to the Phoenix Park, it came back to me: the stench of fresh dung, the strange taste of grass, the sensation of being buried alive.

One afternoon in 1976, I went into the Parkside Hotel beside the gates of the Park. It was a gloomy place then, and the blazing summer sun stopped abruptly at the entrance. I ordered a vodka and found a dark corner to sit in. The place was almost empty and the drone of the afternoon traffic outside made it feel remote and isolated. Two elderly men sat up at the bar, each lost in his own world. One of them looked up every time the number 10 bus passed the window, a vague expression of hope giving way to disappointment. I was so nervous that I could hear the breathing of the old men as clearly as if they were seated next to me. There was something I had to confront in the Park. I had thought about it all that day, had drunk over it in the pubs along the quays. I had been thinking about it for years, but this particular day I had made up my mind to go up there. For what? I wasn't sure. Maybe I would recognise something from the dream.

I drank another vodka – a large one – and this helped me convince myself that I needed to go there to observe, to see, finally, what my monster looked like. I didn't dare think beyond that point. Even the large vodka on top of all the other vodkas couldn't disguise the terror that lay beneath. I would go to the edge and look in. I finished my drink and left the two old men dreaming in the pub. I was so nervous that they seemed to be part of my dream, and the lounge swirled around them and around the fixed and reproving expression on the barman's face. He had read my thoughts, I was sure of it. I could feel his baleful stare burn into me as I hurried out into the sunlight. *He's going into the Park*, he was thinking.

I walked up the main road, past the zoo and over to the cricket grounds, where families sat on the grass watching the matches. The players were all young men in immaculate whites, bronzed and healthy-looking, as if they had been transported from some English film of the 1930s. They exuded that Protestant air of relaxed superiority – still prevalent in the 1970s – as they batted on the scorched grass. A few young working-class men lounged outside the boundary ropes. They looked on with the dull, slightly glazed look of permanent outsiders. Just across the path from the cricket grounds was another world altogether. Here was the Dog Pond, shadowed by trees and so always in darkness. It was as familiar as my own back garden.

There were figures loitering behind trees and bushes. One man got out of his car and walked tentatively into the gloom. Another, younger man appeared, and seemed to beckon him over. They disappeared into a clump of bushes. Nobody at the cricket match was remotely aware of this dark theatre unfolding so close by. I drifted towards the Dog Pond, legs shaking, mind spinning, stomach heaving between desire and revulsion. It was cold out of the sunlight. I sat on a bench and waited. A middle-aged man in a T-shirt threw a stick into the pond, and his dog swam out to retrieve it. The man, like the spectators at the cricket match, seemed unaware of what was going on around him.

Then I saw a group of men at the far end of the pond, huddled outside the public toilets. I wanted to move closer but I was quaking with fear. The man with the dog seemed to be watching me. There was disgust in his eyes. He called the dog out of the water and moved off towards the cricket grounds. The dog refused to follow. The man turned around and screamed abuse at the animal, but I felt that he was really screaming at me, in hatred. Then a car stopped just outside the railings, behind me. I was too scared to look round. I heard the car door open and then shut. Somebody walked across the grass. The dog came out of the pond, shook itself and ran off to its owner. I looked up. A pleasant-looking man of about thirty smiled and nodded towards the toilets. I followed him. He occasionally looked back to see if I was still behind him. He went into the toilet and two other men rushed in after him. I dared not go into that place.

There were six or seven men, young and old, loitering outside, silently eyeing up each other. I walked past them, desperately putting on a brave air and pretending that I wanted to use the place as any innocent passer-by would. Inside, a galaxy of eyes peered out from the dank and smelly darkness. The men looked dirty. Some of them looked like winos. Even the young ones had the grey pallor of people who never see daylight. In one of the cubicles, there seemed to be an orgy going on. About five men were heaving about in the darkness. The man I had followed was at the centre of this activity. He gestured to me to join in. One elderly man was masturbating him while the others jostled to grope at him from behind. What I recall now is the intensity of something that was appallingly out of control. I can still see every detail, catch that awful stench, see those contorted faces of old and young men, gasping and leering as if in some *danse macabre*. I ran out into the fresh air. I was aware of a sudden scurrying in the bushes. The others outside had disappeared. A car revved up and sped away. And then I saw the park ranger approaching the toilet. He looked at me long and hard and then brushed past, muttering those terrible words: 'Filthy queers.'

The journalist Con Houlihan once described the *Irish Press* as a village. Working there in the 1970s and 1980s, it felt like a village in the Valley of the Squinting Windows. Everybody knew everybody else's innermost secrets, and as the paper began to lose its old identity, with the passing of the de Valera generation, cynicism flooded into the vacuum. The unions were in permanent conflict with the management, who were in permanent conflict with themselves. The owner, Major Vivien de Valera, was something of a benevolent despot: kindly, eccentric, but still a despot, and unable to see that the old empire was crumbling. He was encouraged in his delusions by his underlings, as craven a bunch of courtiers as the crowd who had propped up the regime of the mad Emperor Caligula.

Down at our level on the subs desk, the disease spread untreated. Nobody liked the place or had any confidence in its future. Even the feature articles which the three papers published were symptomatic of a creeping paralysis of the spirit. Nostalgia pieces were commonplace. We were always digging up the so-called good old days, as if we needed to look to the past for reassurance. It was not surprising that the most talented people got out. They had seen the writing on the shabby green walls of the old Tivoli Theatre.

Life in the village became oppressive and invasive. We thrived on gossip and trivia. I sat tight, deluding myself that the details of my life were a secret. There were some gay people in the *Press* but they were entombed in their closets, coming out tentatively and only when drunk, to reveal a glimpse of their real selves. One token gay was a senior executive, a figure of malicious fun. He was talented but he never progressed to the top – because of his sexuality, it was assumed. The stories told about him were legion. Most of them were outrageous inventions, but few *Press* people then were prepared to stand between a good story and the truth. One story, which may have contained a germ of truth, had him groping a docker in the toilets behind the Front Office when a cleaning lady interrupted them. 'Jesus, Mary and Joseph,' she yelled, 'Youse are worse than bleedin' Balubas.' After a lifetime as the butt of office jokes, this gentleman retired and was never spoken of again.

The more I buried myself in this world of delusion and cruelty, the more I drank. Alcohol made life bearable: drunkenness sedated the disgust of living the life of a freak. Because I hated the fact of my sexuality, I denied it, even to myself. I could observe other gay people from a distance, becoming a kind of peeping Tom. Sometimes, when I was drunk enough, I would sneak into Bartley Dunne's pub in South King Street, a known haunt of gays, theatrical types, criminals and what passed for the Dublin bohemian set. The place exuded a seedy air. I would sit in a corner and observe the manic swirl. Drag queens, priests, policemen, judges, doctors – all lived out their fantasies there, knowing that just beyond the front door was a hostile world. Homosexuals were regularly beaten up by gangs of 'queer-bashers' and were still persecuted by the authorities.

I was down in the District Court one morning when a strange hush descended upon that normally chaotic place. Two men in their twenties were being prosecuted for 'gross indecency'. The prosecuting guard had apparently witnessed them having sex in their car on Dollymount Strand. I can still see the look of brutish contempt on the judge's face as he asked the defence barrister for 'psychiatric reports' on the two young men. 'Ah Jesus,' I heard a woman in the public gallery mutter in disgust. The very sight of two gay men was too much for her. The hate was tangible and frightening. Though a few brave souls did 'come out' – actors and writers, mainly – the instinct to survive meant that most gay people were forced to lead their lives in fearful secrecy.

One day, not long after the experience in the Phoenix Park, I heard a sudden whisper of outrage in the office. I looked up, to see the editor staring over at me. There was disgust in his face, a mixture of shock and disappointment.

This moment had to come. I had dreamed about it, the terrible moment when the truth about me would blow up out of a normal day. I experienced a weird sense of déjà-vu as I saw the faces of the editor and the crime reporter, Joe Collins, distorted with revulsion. 'He's fucking sick,' the editor said directly to me. I thought of the park ranger and wondered if he had seen my picture over some article of mine in the newspaper and had reported me to the police. I turned to Adrian McLoughlin. Did he know what was going on? He was humming to himself – a nervous, evasive tactic. I suspected that he had had wind of something. Later, in the pub, my suspicions were confirmed.

'Am I in some sort of trouble?' I asked him.

He laughed. 'If you keep coming in drunk, what do you expect?'

'Real trouble?'

He gave me a funny look. He seemed to be scared of something. 'What do you mean?'

I blubbered something about a police investigation.

'Oh that,' he said dismissively, and laughed again.

'What's it about?'

'Nothing.' I knew he was lying. More troubling still, he seemed to be lying in order to protect me.

'There's something going on. I know. I heard what the editor was saying about me today.'

'You heard what?' Adrian asked with a sigh.

'He said that I was sick, a pervert, and that the police were after me.'

He stared into his pint. 'Not at all. You only imagined it.'

The barman in the Scotch House was furiously wiping a pint glass. There was some connection between his jerky, bad-tempered movements and Adrian's nervous attempts at reassurance. I stared at the barman. Did he know something too? As if he was reading my thoughts, he turned suddenly to Adrian to ask him an innocuous question about a soccer match which had been shown on television the previous night. Yes, of course he knew. Everybody knew!

That night, I couldn't sleep. I could see policemen at the front door: middle-aged men in shabby clothes with country accents, threatening and leering. I could see the court, hear the gasps of family and friends as details of an orgy in the Park were read out by an appalled prosecution counsel. I could see the judge, his red face bloated with outrage.

I reached for the naggin of vodka which I had concealed under the mattress for rough nights, and drank it down in one go. The relief was momentary. All too soon, the room was moving again, and strange shapes were forming on the bedroom wall. They were wigs. They ran up the wall like furry little animals. Sometimes they opened out like flowers, one after the other, in slow motion. Then one monstrous wig, a huge yellow spider, climbed up the wall, emitting a horrible stench. It dragged itself into a tiny hole in the ceiling. I lay on the bed in a sweat, my whole body trembling. Only alcohol would make these abominations go away. I licked the mouth of the vodka bottle for a trace of alcohol, but there was no relief. My heart began to pound in my chest. The smell in the room was becoming nauseating, as if dead rats were decomposing behind the wallpaper. I closed my eyes and crawled under the blankets, and then remembered the half-bottle of brandy hidden in the wardrobe.

During the next couple of days in the *Press*, I watched everyone. I eavesdropped on conversations about me, sifting through acres of small talk for the sign that would confirm my suspicions. I spent ages sitting in the loo waiting, listening. Then one day, when the first edition came out, there was great guffawing about the desk. 'Jeremy Thorpe is making a comeback,' a sub called Watkins said, pointing to a story in the paper. Somebody moaned facetiously 'Ooh, sore thing', and Watkins minced around the desk, imitating a camp character in the popular television series *Are You Being Served?* I pretended to join in the fun, hoping that this might force someone to reveal something more substantial than hints or suspicious looks. Watkins continued his pantomime about the disgraced British Liberal Party leader. Everyone at the desk was in hysterics, but their laughter was forced and insinuating. I disliked Watkins. He was priggish and had reptilian eyes.

'Are they jeering at me?' I asked Adrian.

'Everything doesn't have to be about you,' he snapped.

I decided that I wouldn't ask any more questions. I would bury my head in the noise of the *Press* and silently winkle out the truth.

On another afternoon in the lovely summer of 1976, I was sipping a pint of lager in the back of Mulligan's when I overheard two *Press* reporters having an excited conversation. They were behind a partition and so were out of my view, but I could catch bits of their mumbled exchanges.

'As God is my witness, it's true,' Mick Barlow said.

'I don't believe it,' the other replied. (I think he was a junior reporter called 'Squirty' Farrell.)

'But it's all over town,' Barlow insisted.

'When are they going to arrest him?'

I didn't get Barlow's exact reply but I did hear the word 'trap'. He uttered it with malicious relish.

They were talking about somebody whom they both knew well. That somebody had to be me.

Then I heard Barlow more clearly. 'His poor father will die,' he said.

I couldn't listen to any more. I gulped down my drink and ran from the pub, across Butt Bridge, around Liberty Hall and up Abbey Street to the Flowing Tide. Many actors drank there. I needed to hide behind their hysteria, to think, to plan, to get drunk without any more distractions. So I was not imagining the whole thing, after all: they *were* talking about me. They thought I was one of that sordid gang in the Park. And now they were preparing a trap for me. *What kind of trap?* I wondered, as I searched the dark and smoky lounge for a seat. Maybe the Park was the trap. They were expecting me to turn up there. That gave me some relief: I knew I would never go back into the Phoenix Park.

An elderly Abbey actor was singing an Irish ballad at the bar. I envied him. He didn't have a care in the world. I watched him for a long time, fascinated by the way his eyes spun like little black stars behind his jam-jar spectacles. I focused desperately on those orbs. With enough alcohol and distraction, my mind would find a measure of peace again. When the old actor had finished his song, he grinned foolishly at the woman beside him. She smiled and said 'Very nice'. Then she turned away. This rebuff displeased the old man. His foolishly smiling face was suddenly transformed. He glowered at the woman's back and then furiously struggled down off his stool. 'Fucking cow,' he muttered, stumbling to the door.

Adrian still behaved as if nothing was wrong. Occasionally he would let something, some innuendo, slip, and would then immediately retract it. I despised him for his duplicity, but I went along with the charade, never daring to show my mistrust. I fished in our conversations every day for clues.

One afternoon, I turned on him. 'You know what they are all saying about me, and yet you pretend otherwise.'

He inhaled suddenly and then exploded. 'Isn't it fucking time you saw a doctor?' he shouted. I was sure it was for the benefit of the pub.

'I don't need a doctor.'

'You do. You're hallucinating.'

So that was their plan. They hoped I would see a doctor, be diagnosed as mad, and have a spell in a psychiatric hospital. In that way, the scandal wouldn't come out to ruin my family and embarrass the *Press*. My mind was in such a spin of plots, conspiracies, half-heard conversations and imagined slights that I couldn't think clearly any more. The only escape was a further retreat into alcohol and oblivion. Adrian beat his head with his fist in frustration and said: 'How can I make you believe me?' I thought he was a lousy actor as well.

It wasn't too difficult to go mad in the *Press*. It was generally accepted that the place was already a big lunatic asylum; one more crackpot in the ranks would hardly raise an eyebrow. I tried to contain my madness as much as I could and go through the motions of normal behaviour, despite the tempests raging inside me. The people closest to me merely thought I had got quieter. I lived like a spy in enemy territory, tuned to every sound and movement, eyes forever scanning the faces around me in search of clues. I was absorbed in what I called 'the conspiracy'.

My delusions had not progressed to the point where I had to be locked up, but a few times at this stage they did interfere with my work, often with disastrous consequences. On one occasion, I was conducting an interview with a leading Irish actress in the lounge of the Royal Dublin Hotel when I noticed two men at the bar watching the customers. They had the shifty, rather bored look of Special Branch officers. The combination of west of Ireland accents and cheap Clery's anoraks convinced me that I was right. I couldn't concentrate on the interview, and as the actress droned on and on about her 'seminal performances' I escaped into the vodka: doubles, trebles – as much as I could gulp down. I must have passed out in the middle of her monologue, because when I came to an hour or so later, she had departed. I struggled to my feet, approached the two 'policemen' at the bar and accused them of interfering with my civil liberties.

I can still see their gawping, uncomprehending faces as the porters dragged me unceremoniously to the door. A tabloid version of this story got back to the *Press*. In this version, I had vomited over the actress, made a pass at a policeman, threatened to burn down the hotel and caused a minor riot in O'Connell Street. This was all grist to the

Press mill. The crowd in Mulligan's lapped up every exaggerated detail of the sorry tale. After all, variety turns were to be expected in the old Tivoli Theatre.

Outrageous behaviour was a badge of honour amongst the hacks who drank in the pubs around Burgh Quay. They talked about the legendary adventures of famous office drunks, about the theatre reviewer who had wandered onstage in the Gaiety into a pantomime sketch involving Maureen Potter and Danny Cummins, or the crime reporter who had allegedly assaulted the Mayor of Toronto. The stories were legion, half-myth, embroidered and exaggerated to often ludicrous proportions. But this cycle of mythology helped to sustain the culture of the *Press*. The past was slightly wild, like the old West, and heroic feats of journalism were accomplished by stubbled, half-drunk heroes armed with leaky biros. And as Burgh Quay began to decline, we looked back more and more towards this fabled past. The day that President Kennedy was assassinated was a fixed point in *Press* history. Even at the end of the seventies, they were still talking about the brilliant feats of that day – how the editor had gone into Mulligan's and rounded up a few drunken stragglers to bring out a special edition of the *Evening Press*.

So as my behaviour became more eccentric, I think my colleagues believed that I was merely living up to a grand tradition. Most of the older subs were in a permanent state of intoxication, managing to function on autopilot without getting too noticeably tipsy, at least during working hours. One or two were in a fairly advanced stage of alcoholism and suffered from memory loss and psychotic disorders. It was said that when Major Vivien de Valera first called in to see his staff after he had taken over the *Press*, the entire subs desk was drunk. One by one, the subs keeled over when the great man prodded them.

One afternoon, I was very drunk in the office. The day was spent, as usual, 'slipping in and out' to Mulligan's, so by four o'clock the lights were beginning to go out. There was an elderly casual sub still working away on his own – a little bird of a man called Theo, who whistled whenever he spoke. He also reeked of methylated spirits.

'Theo, did you ever imagine that people were talking about you?'

His eyes glittered with amusement. 'Sometimes.'

'And what do they say about you?'

'Oh,' Theo said thoughtfully, 'all kinds of things.'

'Like what?'

'Well, that I'm dead, for instance.'

'They say that you're dead?' Theo giggled and said 'Yes.' And then, after a short pause, he continued: 'But I know better, don't I?'

I wondered what that sensation felt like. Would they sniff and pass comment on the state of one's decomposition? Would they touch you and say things like 'Yes, he *is* dead.' It didn't seem as bad as my own dilemma. Nobody was accusing Theo of disgusting crimes.

'Do you panic?' I asked.

'Panic?' he whistled. 'You get tired of that too.' And the smile hardened into a rictus in his birdlike face as he returned to subbing some bland rubbish on moving house, for the features page.

His mask was perfect. Yes, of course they thought he

was dead. They rarely looked at him, and whenever they talked about him, it was about a dead man. He could not be hurt by them now: the drinking, the shakes, the sweet odour of meths, the mistakes he made, all were beyond reproach. I could assume such a pose, shut down all emotions, withdraw so far into my bunker that I too might become invisible.

Theo strolled into the office most mornings and quietly took his place at the desk. He rarely, if ever, spoke to anyone. We knew little about him save what our senses told us: that he drank too much and didn't wash too often. But we didn't know who he was inside. We never knew what he thought. He did the cryptic crossword and finished it before anyone else. But he never shared his intelligence. That bright bead was focused always inwards.

Adrian surmised that Theo had a past, that he was a laicised priest. Adrian needed to have a personal grip on everyone. Mysteries bored him. But Theo's behaviour reminded me of the madness of Hamlet, the freedom to be absolutely oneself. I began to ask myself what I really feared. But this was in the moments when my courage was buoyed up by alcohol and I was smarting with defiance, muttering to the shadows that I was innocent of all taint. The sober moments were filled with fear: nameless, indefinable yet overwhelming. The immediate fear was of losing my job – I would have no money for drink – but the deeper fear was so pervasive that it haunted my dreams. It was always there, throbbing away like a chronic ache. It became the foundation of my life, influencing everything I thought and did, incubating my feelings of resentment, hatred, self-pity and despair – all of which would suddenly be transmuted into euphoria when the momentary panic had passed. It never allowed me a moment's peace; it never allowed space for the rational to develop. And so my thoughts raced in all directions at the same time, from one crisis to the next, depriving me of sleep for nights on end. And fear was the source of so much manic energy that I could sit up half the night banging away on my old typewriter, churning out poems, articles and short stories, and drinking copiously. I convinced myself that this was creation, this furious struggle between reality and fantasy. And sometimes a good article or a half-decent poem might emerge from this chaos – and then the delusion was complete.

Theo seemed to be beyond fear. This fascinated me. His eyes were calm and secretive, in spite of his intoxicated condition. I began to observe him more closely. I made a note of all his little rituals at the desk: the apple he brought in every day and cut up into tiny pieces, which he proceeded to chew one by one; the tea bag he salvaged and dried out between two sheets of copy paper. When he edited a story, he was forever rubbing out words and laboriously pasting other words in, patiently annotating and revising, so that the final draft was a mystery of hieroglyphics. His handwriting was tiny but perfect, more suited to a museum than to a busy subs desk, since it was impossible to read without the aid of a magnifying glass. Not surprisingly, he was never given anything of importance to work on. He processed the sludge: the Tidy Towns results, the letters, the fillers that bunged the holes in the pages. This, too, I imagined, was by design: he directed the way they thought about him. He wanted them to leave him alone, so that he could busy himself with the trivia and come and go without being noticed. He sometimes slipped out during the late morning, but nobody heeded his absence.

I decided to follow him one day. He went out through the case room, where the typesetters worked, and down the back stairs. When I got to the back door, there was no sign of him anywhere. Since he obviously had not left the building, the only other place he could have gone to was the machine room in the basement. Had he an old buddy there with whom he sat and shared a naggin of whiskey? It seemed a plausible enough explanation. I rather liked the idea of a benign spirit in the bowels of the *Press* who drank whiskey while the editions ran and who provided sanctuary for the likes of Theo.

I began to change my appearance. I no longer dressed in the bright fashions of the mid-1970s, those skintight flared trousers and see-through floral shirts which I was convinced made people suspicious of me. I wore clothes which were duller, which merged with the greys, blacks and greens of the subs desk. But the delusions continued. Some days might pass and I wouldn't hear a thing, but then waves of whispered outrage would sweep towards me from all sides, as if some shocking new fact of my case had just been discovered. It was impossible to remain calm and detached at those times, so I would dig myself deeper into my trench and blank out everything. I would remain there until a kind word or a friendly gesture tempted me to peep out again.

I now began to feel that Pop was aware of what was going on, because he too was watching me all the time. Once, I noticed a car outside the house with two men sitting in it.

'Those policemen are watching the house,' I said to him.

'I don't think so,' he said patiently.

But how could I possibly have told him about my fears? How could I have edited the story so that there would be no shame in it? Could I have explained to him the feelings that had driven me that time to the Phoenix Park? It was better to say nothing. If he knew and was too upset to tell me, then I would have to get at the truth some other way. I thought that I might hear him divulge something over the phone to one of my brothers. So I started to eavesdrop on him as well, listening at the top of the stairs whenever he spoke on the phone. I hated spying on my own father. It felt creepy and wrong. I wanted to tell him my side of the story, but I could not reveal my innermost thoughts. They were so shameful that I had to deny them to myself. They were an aberration that had crept into my head from a monstrous source.

Did he know that the police were laying a trap for me? I decided that he knew the broad facts of the story, and that the family were shielding him from its full awfulness. Yet still no one accused me of anything outright. My colleagues behaved as if they were part of the conspiracy. There were snide remarks and innuendos, but nothing direct. Whenever I asked Adrian about it, I got an embarrassed denial. It felt as if they were attempting to cover up as much as they could and still maintain a normal relationship with me. What was so shocking about the accusation that I couldn't be told it? Maybe there was more to it than the incident in the Park? I began to trawl back over the drunken years for clues. I wondered had something happened in one of my blackouts. I began to examine the worst possible scenarios, yet this fevered search yielded nothing.

4

Slattery's pub in Capel Street was a regular haunt of early-morning drinkers. At 8 AM, the place was full. The customers looked like off-duty policemen, and when I sat down with my glass of vodka and noticed some of them looking at me, the alarm bells went off immediately. One fellow in particular seemed rather too cheerful. He had a great beery laugh and I was sure he had made an obscene gesture towards me. 'We've got ye, boy,' he seemed to say. I looked at him with as much hate as I could muster. He was the stereotypical gobshite figure whom I could just as well have invented. His huge red turnip face streamed with sweat, and as he laughed I could see right into his mouth – the ugly mucous froth that splashed about his lips, only to be flushed back down again into some intestinal sewer. Middle-aged policemen sometimes develop extraordinary shapes, as if an excess of bile is pushing them out in all the wrong directions. This man looked like an old balloon: sagging, lumpy, farting. I couldn't take my eyes off his physical ugliness. What sort of mind did he possess? I wondered. His eyes didn't laugh with the rest of his face. Instead, they darted suspiciously like two little worker ants; and when they happened to settle on me, I felt trapped in some disgusting poison. Here was a man who hated my kind.

I drank my vodka slowly. I rather enjoyed staring back at this Neanderthal and creating a background story for him. I decided that he was from Leitrim, from a large farming family of sisters with names like Kathleen and Bridget, that he had a brother in the priesthood, and that his mind was closed tighter than a rabbit trap. Maybe he was in the Vice Squad, the natural sanctuary of such a beast of prey. I visualised his having sex with his wife, who had to be called Aoife, on a Saturday night, doing it the way he had seen the pigs doing it back home. 'Got ye now, girl.'

After another vodka, I reckoned it was time to go across the road to the chemist. I bought a packet of codeine and went to another early house in the markets, where I got more vodka and swallowed the tablets. I repeated this pattern from Capel Street into the city centre and out again to Ballsbridge, going from pub to chemist shop, swallowing codeine and drowning myself in vodka. I don't know why I picked codeine. I suppose I thought it was the strongest non-prescription drug I could get hold of. Bizarre things happened along the way. A tramp ran across Dawson Street furiously waving his rolled-up newspaper at me. 'Devil! Devil!' he screamed. I remember encountering a large group of uniformed policemen outside the Shelbourne Hotel. My crime had become so awful that it required all these people to keep a watch on me, but I wasn't ready for them just yet. I escaped across Stephen's Green to Earlsfort Terrace. At the corner of Leeson Street, I met one of my *Press* colleagues. He urged me to go back with him to the office. I can still see his startled expression as I called him a two-faced bastard.

It was about noon when I got to Baggot Street. Searson's was filled with office workers having their lunch. After I'd had a drink, I felt the familiar waves of recognition and then revulsion coming from one group. The men were laughing but one girl couldn't control her feelings. 'Oh God,' she squirmed, 'that's revolting.'

I approached the girl, who was in her mid-twenties, and asked her, very quietly, if I could talk to her. I was surprised by the friendliness of her reaction, but what surprised me more was that the rest of the group didn't seem to notice me when I joined them. They went on chatting and laughing among themselves, a typical lunchtime crowd of young office workers.

'What you are saying about me is all lies,' I said. 'I'm completely innocent.'

Her eyes popped. She must have thought I was having her on, because she began to giggle and said, a little flirtatiously: 'I'd say you are all right.'

'I am innocent.'

She got a little edgy. 'Are you in some kind of trouble?' she asked.

I excused myself and left. I couldn't take any more of this pretence from people pointing and laughing at me and then denying it to my face.

I remember stumbling out of the pub and hitting the ground, which felt like rubber. The next thing I recall is lying on a stretcher in the casualty ward of the Richmond Hospital. For some reason, I couldn't take my eyes off my shoe. The heel was loose. That was the first message I received when I came to: the heel of my platform shoe was hanging off. Then I was aware of Pop sitting beside the stretcher. He too was gaping at my shoe.

When they had pumped out my stomach, the nurse told me that I would have to stay the night 'for observation'. I felt angry and depressed – cheated, really – because I was still alive. This wasn't supposed to happen. My plan was to drift out in an alcoholic stupor, but now I would have to do the whole thing all over again. Pop touched me on the arm and left. I wanted to tell him I was sorry. I wanted it to be over, for good – his suffering as much as mine – but I couldn't find the words. Two orderlies wheeled me into the lift.

'Am I going to an isolation ward?' I asked. They ignored me, as if I had not spoken. I realised that sometimes I only spoke in my head.

When we got to the ward, the other patients were sitting by their beds watching me. I was sobering up. I remembered seeing a newspaper somewhere earlier in the day. My photo was on page one, under the headline 'Journalist at Centre of Vice Probe'. It was out in the open at last. One of the patients slammed his newspaper on his locker and spat into his handkerchief. I sank into the bed and listened to the horrible whisperings around me. During the night, I overheard a strange conversation between two doctors who were sitting behind a screen beside my bed.

'I've never seen anything like it,' one said in a shocked voice.

The other said, 'Christ, who would believe it, in this day and age?'

When they went away, I heard another voice reciting the names of all the states in America, over and over again in a dull monotone. This seemed to go on for the whole night. I was convinced that there was much more to the story than I had hitherto believed. Not only was I a notorious pervert, I was also dying of some unspeakable sexual disease, the likes of which hadn't occurred in modern times. I wondered was it syphilis, but that surely would not have provoked such horrified dismay. I vaguely remembered a story by Guy de Maupassant about a young woman dying of such an illness in an isolation ward. I couldn't think of the name of the story. It was just an image of white sheets and an appalling stench. I couldn't think of anything for any length of time because all sorts of shocking revelations about me were flashing to me out of the night. All the whispers and disgusted looks were beginning to make sense. The fact that my friends couldn't tell me what was wrong began to make sense too. I was some kind of plague. The infection of the mind, those dreadful thoughts that I had for so long tried to contain, had now spread right through me.

A doctor came to me in the morning. He seemed kind and normal. I was surprised by this. I told him that I wanted to leave. He said that that would not be a good idea.

'Why? Because I have a disease?'

He paused and, in a low voice, said: 'I think you should go into St Patrick's Hospital. You need help.'

So that was how they were going to get rid of me. They would dump me in the back ward of an asylum and let me rot away. Out of sight, out of mind.

I lied to the doctor. I promised him that I would go over to St Patrick's that day. They reluctantly gave me my clothes.

When I was leaving, an elderly man in the bed opposite smiled and said 'Good luck.' I was elated. I wanted to believe that he was real and that everything else was a delusion. Then he turned to his neighbour and said, 'We're all God's children.'

It was raining outside and my shoe leaked as I trudged home. A man and a woman approached me in Manor Street. I could hear her saying to him under her breath, 'Don't say a word', and as they passed, he said, 'The rain really brings out the dirt.'

The rest of the day passed in a fog of panic, relieved only by alcohol. Yet, even in this state, I could still just about grasp a certain perverse logic to it all. I kept telling myself that I still didn't have complete evidence that my 'delusions' were real. Yes, I heard the voices, saw people's reactions to me, felt their disgust, but could I still be hallucinating, as people said I was? Had I really seen that story in the newspaper? These doubts provided the only hope that was left in my darkening world.

The following morning, I got up when I heard Pop going out to Sunday Mass. I had made my mind up once and for all, and without deliberating any further, I came down the stairs to the kitchen and went straight to the old gas oven. I switched on the gas and put my head inside. After a while, I felt silly lying there on the cold kitchen floor. Then it occurred to me that the meter was empty. I knew that if I started looking for a shilling, I would change my mind again. I laughed at the absurdity of the situation I was in. My knees and back ached and, although I had suicide on my mind, I stood up to ease the pain. I went up to the bathroom. I thought that if I filled the bath full of water and knocked myself unconscious on the bath tiles, I would drown peacefully. I banged my head on the bath and water splashed all over me. Yet I remained conscious – so alert, in fact, that my senses seemed to take everything in with a heightened intensity. The water stung my eyes and nose. I could hear my heart as if it was a football bouncing off my chest. The brown stains in the bath looked like butterflies struggling under the water. I got worried about the house being flooded, so I decided to abandon that course of action. I returned to the kitchen and got a carving knife out of the drawer. I had the blade poised to stab myself in the stomach, hara-kiri style, but my hand was locked on the handle and refused to move. It was getting late. Pop would be returning soon, and I could feel the alcoholic withdrawal starting. I had to postpone the suicide to go out for a cure.

'Did you hear the news?' Adrian was so excited, he could barely contain himself. 'My book is getting published,' he said with pride. 'And it's an English publisher as well!' There was a great air of celebration in the Scotch House that evening as dockers, actors, printers and reporters toasted Adrian's good fortune. I was happy for him. He really needed this moment in the spotlight: nobody had seriously believed that his book would ever come out. He cried over his drink as his cronies congratulated him.

Even Mick Barlow betrayed a sloppy underside to his

carbuncular self. 'Adrian,' he said, 'I always knew you had hidden depths. And an English publisher too! You are made, man.'

The excitement had a hysterical edge to it, as if Adrian's success had suddenly opened up possibilities for all the others. For years, people had said that he had a whole library of books in his head, but he did not possess the discipline to write them. Now they professed delight in being proved wrong.

The old actor from the Flowing Tide edged into the company. 'Ah, Alfie,' roared Adrian in greeting, and the actor swept his arms around him with an exaggerated theatrical flourish. They were old drinking buddies, and Alfie also had a reputation around town as a boozer. He lived in lodgings in Pearse Street but spent most of his life drinking in the pubs of Burgh Quay and Marlborough Street and doing the occasional stint in the Abbey Theatre or on Radio Éireann. When Adrian introduced him to me, I saw that he was already drunk. 'Dear boy,' he gurgled, and then kissed me, smacking two slimy fish across my lips.

The celebrations spilled over into Groome's Hotel. Groome's was opposite the Gate Theatre and was frequented by politicians, journalists, theatre people and, sometimes, the IRA. It was presided over by a charming woman called Patty Groome whose husband was a fundraiser for Fianna Fáil. Most of the serious late-night drinking went on in a shabby back room that had an enormous wall-sized mirror. A naked hundred-watt bulb cast a harsh light over everything. Alfie sat down beside me, and it wasn't long before his hand began to stray. The jam-jar spectacles steamed up as he puffed and giggled, spraying whiskey on everyone within range. Even when his hand was exploring my leg, he was belching rage at journalists in general and critics in particular. He recalled that I had once given him a bad review, and proceeded to berate me in language that would make a navvy blush. I saw Adrian nudge Barlow. I sensed that it was a set-up.

'Piss off,' I said at last to Alfie, and then the storm burst in earnest.

He rose from his seat, took an agitated step backwards and puffed his cheeks out like a bellows. 'I know what you are!' he screamed. 'A cheap little *Irish Press* tart, two fuck-ing mincing steps above the bum boys of Burgh Quay.'

This tirade elicited a roar of laughter from the other drinkers. I could feel my face burning. I wanted to lash out at the old ham, but his remarks had the desired effect, and I crumbled before him. 'Now,' he leered, 'give us a kiss.'

There was no place to hide. He came at me again, his lips protruding like a clam. I endured his horseplay for a few moments and then roughly pushed him off, saying 'Now fuck off.' This provoked applause. Alfie bowed with mock graciousness and slumped back into his chair, mut-tering 'Bitch' as he did so.

Groome's should have been a sanctuary, but it wasn't. I withdrew into myself as waves of hate raged around me. Politicians and actors glowered at this obscene creature in their midst. I gulped down neat vodkas to calm the pandemonium in my head.

Adrian and I got a taxi outside Groome's at about 3 AM. When we got to his house in Drumcondra, he in-sisted that I come in to meet his mother. I could see her face in the dark hallway, terrified of what condition he might be in.

'Why do you think everyone's talking about you?' he asked in the kitchen after his mother had gone up to bed, satisfied that her son was safe, for that night at least.

'They think I'm a queer.'

'Ah, I see. And are you?'

'Certainly not.'

He didn't believe me. He grinned foolishly as he took his dinner out of the oven and said: 'It doesn't bother me, anyway.'

I heard the change in his voice. He was nervous about something. He stabbed at the peas on his plate, burned to tiny buttons after a night in the oven.

'There's a bit of it in all of us,' he said awkwardly.

The atmosphere was suddenly heavy and oppressive. And despite his being so drunk, he still blushed with embarrassment as his real feelings began to show through.

'I hate fucking queers,' I said. I wanted to clear the air immediately, to banish any lingering suspicion that hung over his every laboured word. He looked up from his burnt dinner as if I had just stuck a knife in him. 'They're not all like Alfie,' he murmured, as he tried to cut a piece of charred meat.

I felt sorry for him, for his awkwardness. His sexuality was probably even more deeply repressed than mine. But even now, as he fumbled painfully to find some kind of expression of his feelings, I backed away, slammed an iron shutter down on the conversation. It was safer, I felt, to keep denying everything.

Adrian pushed his dinner aside and lit a cigarette.

5

As the delusions got more and more bizarre, family and friends pressed me to see a doctor. Eventually I decided to visit a psychiatrist in St Patrick's Hospital, but when the afternoon of the appointment came, I panicked. What if they decided that I was mad and needed to be locked up? During my childhood, I had heard stories about Grangegorman, that grim institution off the North Circular Road which we passed on our way to school. Sometimes, I heard terrible screams coming from its grey Victorian interior. The belief was that once people went into a place like that, they never came out.

I sat in the lounge of the Ashling Hotel in Parkgate Street drinking vodka and pondering the terrors that St Patrick's had in store for me. It was a forbidding place, surrounded by a high wall, behind which men and women wandered. I sat in the hotel all evening. I have the vaguest memory of someone calling 'Last orders' and a porter leading me to the door. Then I was walking up the hill to the hospital. The gates were shut. I don't know why I decided that I needed to see a doctor after all, despite the fearful consequences. I was so drunk, I couldn't distinguish between day and night. It seemed the most normal thing in the world to climb over the gate into the hospital grounds. And then, when I found that the front door of the hospital was bolted, I decided, with similar logic, to climb over the roof and scale down the inside wall to the quadrangle, where, no doubt, the nurses would find me and provide sanctuary for the night. I plunged into darkness. Before I lost consciousness, I recall someone peering out from a lighted window. I thought that it was a big red-faced woman and that she was baking a cake.

The following afternoon, I came around in the Meath Hospital. My arm and leg were in traction, and I was being wheeled out of theatre. The young doctor beside the stretcher seemed to be enjoying my predicament. 'You're the first patient I ever heard of trying to break *into* a mental hospital.' They put me in a bed in the public ward, which was to be my home for the next six weeks.

My first concern was how to get a drink. I was bedbound and had only one free hand, but the need for alcohol was paramount. My whole system craved it. I noticed the elderly man in the bed opposite. He lay there like a statue, but I could have sworn that the statue moved. Since I had nothing else to do but lie in my crib, I watched that old man for an entire day for the merest sign of movement. Then, as the visitors were leaving in the evening, I saw the tiniest movement of his hand down the side of his bed. His blank eyes were fixed on the ceiling and only his left hand showed any sign of life. I watched, fascinated. It took nearly two hours for his hand to inch down the side of his bed to his locker. The hand then grasped what looked like a Baby Power. Then the laborious struggle upwards began. He inched the bottle up the side of the bed, across his chest and up to his mouth. A nurse saw what was happening and there was a sudden kerfuffle as she and two of her colleagues tried to prise the bottle from the poor fellow's mouth. The knowledge that his locker contained alcohol cheered me considerably. I lay back in my bed, my mind racing with excitement as I began to plan my immediate future.

The man in the bed beside me was a retired policeman. Last thing at night, he opened his locker and poured himself a small whiskey. I thought of asking him for a drop, but one glass would not suffice. I needed the entire bottle to sustain me, while I planned the means of getting another bottle, and then another. I couldn't think of anything else. My broken leg and arm, work, my father, clean pyjamas, toiletries – all these matters would be looked after once I had arranged a steady supply of alcohol.

On the second day, good fortune played right into my hands. My neighbour was brought down for his operation. When he had gone, I put into practise the strange ritual that I had observed across the ward, taking hours to direct my right hand to feel its way down the side of the bed, then stretch across to the adjoining locker, open it and feel around inside until I had found the bottle of whiskey. I was amazed by how easily the exercise was accomplished. I hid the bottle under the covers, where, out of sight, I had all the time in the world to open the top. I then swallowed two mouthfuls of the neat alcohol and felt life shuddering back into my body. This was heaven. The ward seemed to float around me.

A boy of about sixteen was standing at the end of the bed laughing his head off. 'You're some mover,' he said.

He had a cheeky face. I gestured to him to be careful in case a nurse should overhear. 'Don't worry, the coast is clear,' he said, as he sat down on the stool beside my bed. He introduced himself as Terry. 'It's fucking dead in here,' he said. I knew that he wanted me to help him liven up the place. Then he jumped up again, went over to his own locker and returned with an empty lemonade bottle. 'I'll pour it in for ye,' he said, as he deftly poured the whiskey into the bottle, casting the odd glance over his shoulder for the nurses, who seemed to be busy in the nursing bay at the end of the ward. This kid exuded street wisdom. I liked him immediately and knew that he would be a useful companion. 'I saw yer hand going down to the locker,' he said. 'I didn't think you'd make it, because the nurse almost caught ye.' When he had finished, he poured me a glass of whiskey, humming mischievously as he did so, then placed the bottle inside the locker. 'See, they'll think it's orange squash,' he said, delighted to be part of a conspiracy.

That evening passed in a pleasant alcoholic forgetfulness as the lad, Terry, chatted away about his appendicitis, the other patients in the ward and anything that came into his head. He just needed the company of someone near his own age. In gratitude, he poured me drinks – and promised to get me more when they allowed him out of the ward. He was impressed by my stories of drunken adventures, particularly the one about falling off the roof of the hospital, and I could see that his plans for livening up the ward began to focus upon the ready availability of alcohol.

There was an inquiry next day about the missing

bottle of whiskey. Its owner unfortunately had not survived the operating table, and his grief-stricken daughter was horrified that anyone could have stolen his whiskey in such circumstances. Naturally, the ward sister wanted to get to the heart of the matter. Since I was bed-bound and crippled, I think I avoided coming under suspicion. And Terry, as resourceful as the Artful Dodger, volunteered the fiction that a visitor had been acting suspiciously near the poor man's locker. I felt no remorse, but the experience did teach me to be careful. I planned all sorts of subterfuges for the days ahead, paying Terry to get supplies of whiskey and vodka from an off licence in nearby Camden Street. I did try to maintain a discreet level of drunkenness, however, lying, half-tight, in the bed and hoping that the nurses wouldn't notice. But then the delusions started again, and before long I was imagining that the other patients were planning to murder me. I strained my ears to hear their conversations, my free hand clutching the bottle under the sheets in anticipation of a sudden assault.

One Saturday night, I was convinced that the patient opposite was talking about me to his family. Occasionally, one of his visitors would cast an outraged glance in my direction. I drained off a Baby Power and then lobbed the empty bottle across the ward. The bottle smashed off the wall behind the man's bed, and shards of glass showered down on his family. The last thing I remember was a young Indian doctor giving me an injection, with Terry in the background jumping with excitement.

I must have been unconscious for many hours, because the next morning the Sister was standing over me and saying that any further incidents would get me transferred to Grangegorman. Pop was called in and was told that I was a dangerous patient. He looked down at me in despair. The nurses gave me medication to get over the worst symptoms of alcohol withdrawal, but no amount of Librium could still my hallucinations. I could no longer distinguish between fantasy and reality as I lay there, for days, suspended between two worlds. Even Terry was frightened away. Most days, I sweated in terror, my free hand clasping the tin of shaving foam, with which I would defend myself when they sneaked up to strangle me. Then, late at night, when the visitors had gone and the ward had settled down, I would witness the weirdest scenes at the end of my bed. It seemed as if a troupe of travelling players came into the ward every night to perform the most grotesque and bloody plays. They would dangle human heads, dripping with blood, over my bed. One night, the heads were those of my parents. The actors screamed a strange aboriginal language and from their mouths came a horrible faecal stench as they danced with their frightful booty up and down the ward. The principal actor was an ancient man in a white nightshirt. He was caked in faeces and was constantly tearing up a newspaper to wipe himself and then flinging the filthy papers on to my bed.

One night, a river of faeces crept along the ward. The old man was buried up to his head in the stuff and emitted an ear-splitting shriek as he tried to struggle free. His hand reached my bed and, as he violently pulled at the sheets, I could feel myself slipping into the disgusting lava. I was choking. The shit was clogging up my nostrils.

Hands were pulling at me frantically. Then, just as I felt I was drowning, a huge figure lunged over me and pulled me to safety. It was the night nurse.

One Sunday evening, the miracle happened. I over-heard a mumbled conversation between two patients, one of whom had just been admitted to the ward. He was being given the customary low-down on the other patients. I strained my ears with excitement. Now, at last, I would hear the full truth. I heard some whispered remarks about a patient who had died the previous night. Then, when they got to my bed, I heard the words: 'He's a journalist. He's very quiet.'

These few words provided the one straw that I desper-ately needed. I clung to it tenaciously, sensing that it pointed the way back to sanity. It required an enforced spell of sobriety in a hospital to bring me to the realisation that the whole business about the Phoenix Park, the police, the sexual disease, the article in the paper, was a giant fig-ment of my imagination, just as my family, friends, doctors and nurses had repeatedly said. But I still had my doubts. Some experiences were far too raw and realistic to put be-hind me, and I wondered whether there was some germ of truth, waiting for enough alcohol to create a monster.

But I was now thinking about getting better. In my own mind, the crisis had changed from a criminal to a medical one. The delusions simply stopped, as quickly as they had started. The fog evaporated, and the baleful stares and conspiratorial nudging suddenly faded into the nor-mal behaviour of ordinary people. I must have started to behave normally again, because the other patients began to chat amiably to me, and even Terry wanted to test the hospital's security by trying to smuggle more alcohol in. Were the patients talking about me? I asked him. 'Yeah,' he replied. 'They thought you'd flipped.'

The delusions might have stopped, but I still needed alcohol. I now had another reason for needing it more than ever: the sheer delighted relief from all that mental turmoil. I could not see the connection between my dependence on alcohol and my madness. So I paid Terry to smuggle in a small bottle of whiskey to me every night. I was content with that. I would spend the entire day looking forward to the night's little treat, counting the hours, even the minutes, to the moment when Terry would appear with the naggin concealed in his jacket. Some of the junior nurses turned a blind eye to my renewed drinking. They felt sorry for me, strapped to a bed for weeks, and one of them even said that a drop of the hard stuff at night wouldn't kill me. This was the seventies, after all. Patients still smoked in the wards; some of them even slipped out to the pubs in Camden Street.

Terry kept me company most days, leaving my bed only when a visitor arrived. In his own way, he understood my problem, and, by sneaking in the drink, he did what he considered was the kindest thing to do in the circumstances. Besides, the ward sister and the doctors were the enemy, and he was drawn instinctively to my rebellion. I can still hear him planning to outwit the Sister, the excitement in his voice at the idea of pulling the wool over her eyes. One day, I heard one of the senior nurses giving out to Terry. She scolded him as one might a dog. His eyes watered when she called him 'an ignorant little gurrier' in front of the entire ward, and for a moment his natural resilience left him and he was speechless with hurt and rage. I felt my anger rise. He might have been a rough, un-educated inner-city boy, but he was painfully insecure be-hind his swaggering macho front. I hoped that he wouldn't cry as he tried to shrink away from the gaze of the ward. We never spoke again, because later that afternoon they packed him off to another ward. Even then, I didn't feel that I had betrayed Terry. I just felt growing panic at the thought of not being able to get my supply of alcohol.

The *Press* was responsible for everything that had hap-pened to me; I had to believe that. The *Press* and, beyond it, the repressive society it served, was the natural focus for all my rage and fear. If I didn't believe that, I would have been forced to look inwards and to accept personal responsibility for the way I was living my life. It was in the *Press* that the delusions had started. The moment in the subs room is etched indelibly in my memory. The sud-den startled looks of outrage are as clear and intense as a recurring dream.

When I'd joined the newspaper as a trainee journalist, I had believed that it was an exciting and glamorous place. It was part of Irish history: de Valera, the American money that had helped set it up, its republican ethos, even the old music-hall atmosphere of the building – all these things were hugely impressive to a youngster. And then there were those legendary columnists whose words had informed my childhood: Kevin O'Kelly, whose film re-views opened up Hollywood for me; Gabriel Fallon, who wrote ceaselessly about his friend Sean O'Casey and therefore was a living link to the early Abbey Theatre of Yeats, Synge and Lady Gregory; Brendan Behan, whose voice roared iconoclastically through the place; J. Ashton

Freeman, who wrote so elegantly about wildlife. The *Irish Press* had a reputation as a great newspaper. Its chief rival, the *Irish Independent*, still looked like an Edwardian publication, with its small ads on the front page. But the *Irish Press* was dynamic and had a team of gifted reporters.

But soon the reality hit me like a damp dishcloth, and all that glamour, legend and excitement seemed to shrink into a rather shabby caricature. What shocked me on the first day was the smallness of the place and how dingy it looked. Even the workers seemed bored and had an unhealthy pallor about them; like people who worked down in the mines. The management of the *Press* were villains straight from Central Casting. We made ourselves believe that. An atmosphere of fear prevailed on Burgh Quay and, inevitably, that created chronic drunkenness and periodic madness among the staff – which in turn fed the cycle of delusion. Whatever shortcomings the *Press* management had – and there were many – the insecurity deepened so relentlessly that we felt that the newspaper was doomed. The *Sunday Press* was still the largest-selling paper in Ireland, but the creaks and groans of disaster could already be heard. It had become complacent with success, and by the mid-1970s was losing its way.

Adrian and I did the ten o'clock shift on a Saturday night. We were usually drunk. Sometimes Adrian was so inebriated that he couldn't make it up the stairs to the *Sunday Press*. He slept it off in the toilets and then reported for duty in the small hours, looking like the Ghost of Christmas Past. When we finished our shift at about 2 AM, we went to a late-night pub in Townsend Street and drank until dawn.

When I returned to work on my crutches, the *Press*

was going through one of its periodic convulsions. The row this time was about air quality, so we had regular 'air breaks', when the unions instructed their members to down tools and take a walk on Burgh Quay. The foul air was caused by the building of a new newsroom in the run-down Victorian premises. But management was locked into its traditional posture of denial, insisting that the air in the building was as clear as a fresh morning in paradise – although there was evidence of dangerous levels of asbestos. This arrogant refusal to accept the obvious became a symptom of the terminal decline of Burgh Quay.

Despite the unruly state of relations between labour and management, the personnel manager at the time (they came and went as if through a revolving door) began to take an interest in my 'illness'. I remember hobbling into his little office as he was furiously scratching away at a memo. 'How are you?' he said, without looking up, and in the tone of an army surgeon inspecting a victim of trench foot. I was obviously part of that vague workers' plot that was undermining his little fiefdom. He looked at my crutches with distaste.

'It is my duty to warn you,' he said, 'that if there are any more "scenes" while on duty, we shall have to seriously consider firing you.'

'What scenes?'

'You've been reported drunk on duty five times in the past six months.'

Since this interview took place during an 'air break', I went out to the pub when it was over. Two hours and half a dozen vodkas later, the voices were again whispering in my head. All my rage at the *Press* erupted that afternoon in

Mulligan's. That crowd, I told myself, had taken away my youth, my sanity and now my ambitions. I had wanted to be a feature writer but they had insisted that I remain on the subs desk, pasting down and cutting up, shovelling the shit into the great public maw. I had wanted to be a reporter, to be out and about in the real world, but no, management decided that I was too unstable to be dealing with real people. So I was consigned to this elephants' graveyard. I could write the occasional feature article, but they had to be safe, nostalgic pieces. They had to be about the past, where I could do no harm.

I went back into the office, drunk on my crutches. Watkins was watching me. He nudged John J. Dunne and whispered some sarcastic remark. John sniggered ingratiatingly. Watkins should have been a clerk in a tea company, but his conspicuous mediocrity had already attracted management's attention, and so he was now being groomed for promotion. I felt strangely calm. I knew what had to be done. I sat with my head buried in the morning paper and waited patiently until old Theo got up to move. I followed him down to the works. It was like a mine shaft down there, with production workers milling in and out of dark recesses. Theo disappeared as usual into a tiny ante-room. Then I saw my opportunity. A man was siphoning oil into a canister from a drum. I breezed up to him with my mug and asked him for some, lying to him that my car wouldn't start.

I went back up to the newsroom and into the men's toilets. They were empty. I picked a cubicle. The morning paper lay open on the floor. 'Don't think,' I said to myself, over and over again. I'm sure I said it aloud. I doused my clothes with the oil, then my hair, shoes, face – every part of me. I kept thinking of the calm expression on that Vietnamese monk's face as he burned to death on a crowded street in Saigon several years before. It would be over in seconds; just a swoosh, and then silence. I dared not think of the pain. The sweet stench of the oil made me giddy. This was the very edge. I sat down on the toilet seat and tried to control my furiously shaking legs. I told myself that I needed a drink first. No, I reasoned, I had gone too far. I couldn't leave this cubicle covered in oil. I impulsively struck the match. It didn't light. I stared at the floor, waiting for the explosion. The paper was open at the small ads. There were hundreds of humble requests in tiny black print for second-hand lawnmowers, prams, pianos, mattresses – the bric-a-brac of ordinary lives. I envied this normality. The morning's drink was dying in my system. I badly needed a fix. Yet if I didn't strike another match, I'd lose my nerve. The thought of going back out to that horrible whispering, covered in oil and full of shame, was unendurable. I struck another match. That one didn't light either. There was just a sudden acrid stench. My hands were so sweaty that the box of matches had gone damp. I remembered the lighter. Just as I reached into my pocket for it, the cubicle door burst in on me. I saw Adrian first, then John J. Dunne and Watkins, but it was old Theo who seemed to be in control. He grabbed the box of matches from me as the others dragged me from the cubicle. Theo was quite calm. He was the only one who spoke. 'Wash him down first,' he ordered, and Watkins started to scrub my face and hair with a wet rag.

'You mad bastard,' Adrian said, catching his breath at

last. 'Do you want to blow up the whole of Burgh Quay?'

Someone else came into the toilets. I caught a glimpse of a shocked face. 'It's all right,' Theo muttered, and whoever it was beat a hasty retreat. They escorted me out, through the newsroom and down the stairs to the front office, where Adrian and John pinioned me to a chair while Watkins rang for a taxi.

'I'm not going home,' I protested.

'No, you're going to the hospital. And no messing this time.' It was the editor, white as a ghost. The four of them surrounded me, and I knew that any further protest was useless. All I could hope for was a huge dose of sedatives when they got me to the hospital.

6

The motto over the entrance to Dean Swift's hospital reads: *Festina lente*. Hasten slowly. When I stepped into the mid-eighteenth-century gloom, everything had slowed down; it was a dreamlike place. Patients drifted along the endless corridors, white eyes turned inwards. They were like a race of people trying to grope their way back to some dimly remembered homeland. Everywhere was this startled yet trancelike movement. A young woman with Bette Davis eyes slumped past me. A cheerful young male nurse accompanied me up a staircase which had high railings to prevent inmates from throwing themselves over it. Puffing from the climb, he made a joke about not being fit. We came to Ward 3 B, a long dormitory with rooms off it, which contained the most seriously disturbed male patients. The walls were yellow and vaulted. A stench clung to everything: clothes, bedlinen, and nurses and patients alike. A cleaning lady with violently dyed red hair was polishing the lino floor, but it was a useless task because the dank odour was overwhelming. Occasionally, she would rest from her labours and drag on a wet stump of a cigarette. She looked vaguely like the drag artist Danny La Rue.

I couldn't sleep that first night despite the vial of

Largactyl which the nurse gave me. There was too much astir; ghosts drifting down the corridor all night long, wandering in and out of the toilets, wrestling with their bed sheets. I heard the nurses arguing with one patient whom they called 'Mr Manning' and who kept soiling his bed. Every so often, I would hear the nurses rushing to his bed, then the violent flapping of sheets and the old man whimpering in protest as they tried desperately to stem some faecal tide. 'Put a plug in it, Mr Manning,' one young country nurse called out in despair. One man spent the night standing at the end of my bed, staring relentlessly at me. Every time I looked up, there was this moon face with its eerily vacant eyes.

At around 6 AM, I noticed some patients going into the little kitchen off the ward, and I decided to follow them. Inside, it was like a pub late at night. A cloud of cigarette smoke hung over the patients, who had suddenly come alive on their first cup of tea of the day. It was a tiny grey room, just a plastic table and chairs, and a press full of foam mugs and boxes of tea bags. One man, nick-named Fred Astaire, seemed to be in charge. Even in his dressing gown, he looked dapper as he dunked a tea bag into his carton. 'Ah, a new customer,' he said, as he went to fill his mug again.

His sidekick was an older, heavy-set man whom every-one called, deferentially, Mr B. Both, apparently, were per-manent fixtures of the ward. Mr B. had a melancholy, polar-bear face which gazed into some white wilderness. He was quite big and rough, yet there was something fem-inine about him too, particularly around the eyes. His dressing gown was wrapped tightly around him like a bandage.

When I introduced myself as a drunk, the group seemed quite relieved. There was a pecking order, with the alcoholics on top and the manic depressives and schizophrenics very much at the bottom of the pile. The morning tea club consisted exclusively of alcoholics, though some of them were by now obviously brain-damaged.

'Well, I'm glad you're not one of them head cases,' Fred said. I noticed that most of his teeth were gone. 'They shouldn't be here at all.' He had an effeminate Dublin accent pitched towards mock outrage.

'You're too young to be in here. Go home,' Mr B. roared. Fred winked at me. 'Don't mind him, son, it's the Largactyl.'

'Largactyl me arse,' Mr B. boomed. 'It's living in here with an old faggot like you.' Fred's pink face creased into an angry concertina and I thought he was going to empty his mug of tea over the older man. 'Show us your legs,' Mr B. went on. 'He's got the same legs as Gerty Gitano in the old Tivoli.'

'You remember the Tivoli?' I interrupted. There was a great guffaw from everyone.

'We *were* the Tivoli,' said Mr B. proudly. He and Fred were old music-hall artists.

'Artistes!' screeched Fred.

'And even then,' Mr B. continued, pointing at his pal, 'he was a mad old queen.'

Fred placed the mug on the table, hoisted himself up over Mr B. and, still winking at me, exclaimed: 'If you didn't have me to look after you, you'd have been making baskets in Grangegorman years ago!'

I could see that they played off each other – still the

old comedy duo from the variety theatre of another age. Mr B. grabbed Fred's testicles. 'Show the lad your fucking fanny,' he said, whereupon Fred swirled around and slapped him so hard on the face that Mr B. slumped back again into his chair, stunned.

'I'll fucking fanny you,' Fred snarled, as if he meant it. 'Ye filthy child molester.'

Mr B. grinned foolishly. He knew he was beaten.

Fred was building up a stream of invective, and nothing could stop him now.

'That's why he's in here, ye know,' he said to me. 'Interfering with messenger boys from Dockrell's Hardware Store.' The whole kitchen was laughing now.

'And when he wasn't interfering with them, he was flashing at the young ones in the queue outside the Carlton Cinema.'

'I'll sue you for slander,' Mr B. warned.

'Sue me arse,' Fred shot back. Mr B. said that he was on first-name terms with some of Dublin's leading solicitors. 'The only solicitors you know,' said Fred, 'are two-shilling blow jobs in Benburb Street.' The night nurse looked in and warned them to keep quiet. 'Poor Mr Brennan is trying to sleep,' she said.

'Ah, don't mind Franz Josef,' said Fred, turning to me. 'That oul' fella thinks he's the Emperor of Austria, no less.'

'Well, keep it down anyway,' the nurse replied, with good humour. She turned to Mr B. and told him his sister was coming to visit him that afternoon. I saw sudden fear in his eyes.

'Why, after all these years?' Mr B. said.

'Because it's time,' said Fred, now gentle and re-assuring. The kitchen went dead quiet.

'She's up to something,' said Mr B., clearly fretting.

Breakfast consisted of porridge, brown bread and a fry of bacon, sausages and two greasy eggs. Fred invited me to share his table with Mr B. and Franz Josef, a huge man with a handlebar moustache and staring eyes. Sometimes he shouted battle orders to imaginary soldiers in the ward. Fred said he was still suffering from shell-shock from the Great War. Franz Josef had fought in the Korean war, but Fred had no sense of time. Seagulls swirled and screamed outside the dining-room window, their furious red eyes demanding leftovers, which the patients threw to them. Occasionally, a patient would toss his tablets to the gulls; uppers or downers, the birds didn't seem to mind.

That first morning on the ward seemed interminable. After breakfast, I was told to go back to bed to await further sedation. When the doctors had finished their rounds, a dull, echoing silence descended, broken only by the whispering of patients and the perpetual rattling of keys as nurses opened and locked the main door of the ward.

I noticed one particularly strange-looking man with a huge mole on his left cheek. He was the patient who had stood staring at me throughout the night. He was wandering down the ward, eyes watching every bed. I knew he was a sex maniac. The ceaseless and helpless lust in his eyes told me that. Sex maniacs in those days were supposed to have a certain look. In the darkness, he had seemed vacant. Now he was apparently in the throes of some irresistible sexual drive, searching, touching shapes in the beds, whimpering whenever a nurse told him to go back to his room. He caught me looking at him. A strange smile crept slowly up his face and, licking his lips, he lunged towards my bed and grabbed my leg. The movement was so sudden and predatory that for a moment I was frozen, mesmerised by the way his reptile tongue rattled excitedly in his mouth.

'Harold, behave yourself,' Fred shouted, pushing him away from my bed. Harold relaxed his grip and squirmed in rage like a child when Fred called the nurse to take him back to his room.

'That's only Harold. He's harmless really,' Fred chuckled, sitting down by the side of the bed.

'Harmless!' I shouted.

Fred was wearing make-up and I wondered how he managed to get hold of it. His hair was obviously dyed with henna. It looked red and rusted. Maybe the cleaning lady shared her beauty secrets with him? I liked Fred. There was something endearing about him, the way he mothered everyone. 'I'm worried about Mr B.,' he said. Already he was confiding in me. This was to become a regular feature of life in the ward: seeming intimacy – which I had to learn not to trust. Fred was agitated.

'Maggie, Mr B.'s sister – her coming in is bad news, I tell you,' he said. 'If poor Mr B. leaves here, the only place for him is Grangegorman. And he'd die in that hell-hole.'

'But why would he leave?'

'Maggie has had enough. She's been paying his hospital bills for too long.'

Fred stared forlornly down the ward. These old lags were inseparable; a Derby-and-Joan relationship that had survived the Dublin variety years into this institutionalised twilight.

'Why do you call him Mr B.?'

'Oh, he was always Mr B. in the theatre, you know. Larry Byrne is his real name, but he would be offended if you called him that. I hear you work in the *Press*. Ah, the great shows we used to have in that place when it was the Tivoli.'

I pretended to doze off. Fred may have remembered footlights, magicians and clowns, but I thought of the old Tivoli as the source of nightmare. There was no escaping the *Press*, even in the lunatic asylum.

When I saw Maggie that afternoon, I thought she was a man in drag. She was the very image of Mr B. Her eyes were tired and lightless. She marched down the ward clutching her handbag.

'She was a Royalette, you know,' Fred whispered admiringly as she sailed past like some gaudy Spanish galleon. 'The three of us were on the town together,' he said with a hint of sadness.

Maggie spotted Fred. 'Are you still here?' she boomed.

'Hello Maggie,' Fred said nervously.

She came over to the bed to take a closer look at us. The dyed hair, the red lipstick, the way her skirt billowed as she moved, hinted at a lively theatrical past.

'You're still here?' she repeated. The shock of seeing Fred seemed to unwind her and she sank onto the next bed.

'Your brother is waiting for you down in the television lounge,' Fred said.

'Well, let him wait. Haven't I been waiting on him these years past.' She winked at me. 'This pair,' she said to me, 'have ruined my life.'

Fred gabbled some protest, but she turned on him ferociously, her huge black eyelashes fluttering.

'Youse have! For thirty years the pair of you have been hiding away in here.'

'You think I like it here?' Fred shouted.

'Yes,' she rasped. 'First that brother of mine would come in, and you'd be in after him to keep him company. Oh, a right pair of jugglers youse were. And ye left me to fend for meself.'

'Ah now, Maggie,' Fred whimpered.

'Don't "Ah Maggie" me. You were always cowards, afraid to stand up to the real world.'

I could see that Fred was near to tears now. 'He said he was sorry, Maggie.'

She raised her voice even louder and Franz Josef covered himself with his sheets in distress. 'Sorry! It's a bit late for that. My brother would have been all right if you didn't egg him on. He was doing well on the stage, but you had to bring him into the pubs, knowing full well his weakness for the booze. And then when he couldn't get work any more because of the drink, this is where youse ended up. Like the greatest pair of losers since the fiddlers went down with the *Titanic.*'

She was fumbling in her handbag for a packet of cigarettes. She lit one and blew a cloud of smoke contemptuously into Fred's face.

Fred snapped. 'And what about your great plans and schemes that never went beyond closing time?'

She sucked derisively on her Woodbine. 'I never came in here.'

'No, but you drove your brother to the drink with your demands.'

Maggie raised herself off the bed, her red lips curled in outrage. 'What?' she screamed.

Fred was spitting with rage. 'He came in here to get away from your mollycoddling him and smothering him like you were his bleedin' wife.'

She lunged forward. 'Jealous old bastard,' she hissed, stabbing the air with her cigarette. Fred lunged back at her until their faces almost met.

'He had no life because of you,' he said.

I thought she was going to slap him. 'I'm his sister.'

'Well, he couldn't live with you any longer. Any spark he had, you smothered it out of him.'

She blinked defensively. 'I'm his sister,' she repeated. 'I wanted a normal life for him. Not gaddin' about town with a pathetic song-and-dance man like you, being led into improper company.'

Fred jumped up off the chair, screaming like a fishwife. 'Are you saying that I corrupted Mr B.?'

She growled at him, the yellow teeth snapping down on the words like an animal in pain. 'Yes, and you're still at it, thirty years on. Look at him.' She turned to me. 'Still thinking he's Freddy Doyle in the old Tivoli. You were never Freddy Doyle, even then. You were a drunken bowsie with less talent than ye had sense. And now look at ye, an old has-been living on the scraps of an imagined past.' Fred tried to speak, but words failed him.

'Were you on the stage as well?' I asked her.

For the briefest moment, her face lit up. 'Yes, I was.' Her accent changed. She was suddenly posh, almost coquettish. 'In the Theatre Royal. I worked with Alice Delgarno and Babs de Monte.'

When I showed that I was impressed, she blew triumphantly on her cigarette and gathered her handbag. 'I'll tell you, Freddie, I'm not waiting for him to get better again' – and she stormed off towards the television lounge, her head held high.

Fred told me their story. The three of them had belonged to a variety group called 'The Alickadoos', which had played in the Queen's, the Tivoli and the Royal. But when variety died out in the early 1960s, they began to drink more, usually in the Bleeding Horse in Camden Street. They had a ball for a couple of years, but increasingly Mr B. and Fred had to be dried out in psychiatric hospitals. As their alcoholism worsened, their sojourns in hospital began to lengthen, until they became semi-permanent patients. Maggie still drank in the old haunts, maintaining a lonely watch on the past. 'Poor Maggie' was all Fred could say. I felt that he was genuinely sorry for her and regretted whatever part he had played in the way her life had turned out. Had she been in love with him once, I wondered? He must have been a good-looking man in his youth. He was obviously gay, though probably terrified of it. The hospital had become a kind of closet where he, and presumably Mr B., could act out their strange celibate marriage. They seemed to be accepted as a couple by the other patients, their noisy marital rifts turning into ancient music-hall comedy acts. It was impossible to know what was real in this place. Sadness, yes – that was palpable. So too was hysteria. Compared to Franz Josef, Harold and the other patients who drifted perpetually inside their own heads, Fred and Mr B. seemed almost normal. Their conversation sounded like sketches from the music halls as they twittered away in endless circles, increasingly divorced from their real selves, but I felt a deep bond between them that looked like love. Maybe the hospital was the only home they could share, a tentative twilight place for their unspoken needs. I tried not to read too much into their situation because most of what I saw was a production, a stylised version of life, but I could not help feeling that these were gay children of the 1930s and 40s, driven so far underground that nothing existed for them any more but shadow and illusion.

Because I had been plunged into other people's lives as soon as I arrived in the hospital, I had had little time to consider the wreckage of my own life. The panic of the world outside began to recede as the days passed in the foggy turbulence of Ward 3B. Pop came in one afternoon with toiletries and clean pyjamas. He sat beside the bed and observed the strange comings and goings. I think I told him I was sorry for everything that had happened. He just patted my knee. He was embarrassed. Any time I tried to open up to him about my illness, he was uncomfortable. I wondered had the doctors told him the terrible thoughts that were in my head.

'There's nobody talking about you,' he said quietly when I tried to bring up the subject. 'That's all just the drink.'

It wasn't as simple as that, I thought. But I also knew that he couldn't be part of a conspiracy as frightful as the one I had envisioned. That belief was the second straw of hope that I clung to.

After ten days of 'bed rest', I was given back my clothes. I felt a sensation of freedom after being so long in pyjamas and a dressing gown. The stench in the ward penetrated everything – skin, clothes, hair – so that after a few days it became unbearable. Now I could leave the lock-up ward and explore the rest of the hospital.

That first morning I went out to the grounds to breathe fresh air again. It was so beautiful and peaceful, like a monastery garden, with red roses climbing up the hospital's perimeter walls. I came across a croquet lawn bordered by banks of delphiniums. The sweetly perfumed air was a blessing after the dankness of the admission ward. I sat in the mellow early-September sun and tried to remember the lines of a poem by Austin Clarke which I thought might perfectly capture the mood of this garden haven. He had spent some time in St Patrick's Hospital, and the poem 'Mnemosyne Lay in Dust' was inspired by his stay. It was hard to credit that this walled sanctuary was right on the verge of the city, a mere stone's throw from the Guinness brewery and Kingsbridge Railway Station. I thought of the philosopher Wittgenstein sitting here, brooding, in the early 1940s. He was living then in the Ashling Hotel and used to walk up the hill from the river to hear Professor Norman Moore's brilliant talks on the developing science of psychiatry. I thought of the countless thousands of anonymous people who had sought peace here over the centuries – Swift's forgotten race.

Two nurses were leading a patient along the pathway. He was a tall, heavy-set man, and he looked familiar. He was, in fact, an actor from the popular television soap opera *The Riordans*, in an advanced stage of the condition known as Korsakov's syndrome, brought on by alcohol abuse. I had heard Fred talking about the 'wet brains' ward out in the grounds and wondered what horrors it contained.

Piano music was coming from one of the buildings nearby. Somebody was playing 'Shall We Dance?' from the musical *The King and I*. In a window, I could see a young male nurse leading an elderly female patient in a waltz. She had on a party dress and a paper napkin pinned to her hair to create a bow. She was a ghost.

What struck me when I got back to Ward 3B was the grey pallor of all the patients' faces. Even Fred, despite his make-up and tinted hair, looked sickly grey. He was also agitated. I thought it was because of Mr B., but then he told me that he was being transferred downstairs to the place I had just seen. 'They're all demented down there,' he yelled in despair, and then raced off to tell Mr B. his bad news.

That night, the patients held a party in the kitchen as a farewell to Fred. One of them had brought a cake and another had bought lemonade from the shop, but Fred didn't seem to be in the mood.

'He's stuck here in this hospital for good,' Mr B. whispered to me. I could smell alcohol on his breath.

'So you'll be separated?'

'Yeah, thank God, at last,' he replied, trying to hide his distress. 'But maybe I'll go down and visit him when I get me clothes back.'

Where did he get the drink from? I asked him. He pretended not to hear me and, when I pressed him, he turned sour. 'How the fuck could I get drink into this place? It's worse than Alcatraz here.' But I knew that somehow he managed it, and I began to suspect that he had been getting drink in all along. Fred cut the cake and made a little speech thanking everyone for their kindness.

'You're not going to fucking China,' Mr B. shouted.

There was an almighty roar from the ward. 'Ah Jesus,' Fred quipped. 'Franz Josef wants a bit of cake!'

When I went into the ward to investigate, I saw Harold lying on the floor beside Franz Josef's bed. There was blood spurting from his nose, and he was wailing like a castrated donkey. Two male nurses were trying to lift Harold onto his feet while a third endeavoured to restrain Franz Josef, who seemed to be having some kind of fit in his bed. Harold had made a pass at the old man. The commotion died down when the nurses dragged Harold off to his room.

I started to attend group therapy sessions, where we all sat around on cushions in a darkened room. This was called Gestalt Therapy, and the earnest young Canadian therapist, Mr Meeker, urged us to 'open up' to each other – which seemed to be an invitation to indulge in hysteria. A girl called Aileen screamed rage at her cushion and then proceeded to bite and tear it. Apparently she was killing her father. The rest of the group started chanting 'Kill, kill' as she scratched and screamed, before finally collapsing in tears.

'How do you feel now?' Mr Meeker asked her, and she started to scream again.

I was bored. I thought they were acting. In fact, I knew they were, because when my time came to 'open up', I decided to cheat and create a whole new set of demons to replace my real ones. I invented a girlfriend called

Angela. She was the love of my life and we had planned to get married. One night I found her in bed with my colleague and best friend, Adrian McLoughlin. As I rambled on, I realised that nobody was really listening. The members of the group were obsessively preoccupied with themselves, so my performance was futile.

There was another fellow in the group around my own age, and he was unimpressed. His name was Roger and he seemed amused. He listened to every word of my story, obviously not believing any of it. He was as bright as a button – the only sane person in the room. His face had the awful pallor of the mental institution, yet I could see that there was something alive behind his parchment skin – some mischievous spirit, a gremlin maybe.

But the only person in the hospital to whom I could talk with complete freedom was Fred. I used to visit him every day in his new home, the geriatric ward. This place was even grimmer than 3B, though it was a newer building – an extension added to the hospital some years earlier. It was like a monstrous crèche, with walls painted in lurid colours. Some of the patients were strapped into chairs, but the rest of them were in constant motion, and the nurses were exhausted just trying to keep order. There was an art class in session but the patients were throwing the paint around the room. Fred was sitting at an easel desperately trying to ignore the chaos around him. He was wearing a smock and had just started to paint a house.

'I'm not staying here,' he said. 'I told them I was leaving.'

'But where will you go?'

'I could rent a room off Maggie.'

He was serious. As he dabbed paint onto his canvas, I wondered was there method to his madness. If he could persuade Maggie to take him in as a lodger, then Mr B. would have no reason to stay in hospital. All three would be reunited at last.

But I was entering into Fred's delusions. How could he live with Maggie? Had he no idea of the pain and loneliness she had suffered because of him and Mr B.?

'I'm leaving next week anyway,' he said. I began to think that Fred was more disturbed than I had imagined. Why would they put him into this terminal ward otherwise?

'Fred, are the other patients saying things about me?'

'Like what,' he said warily.

'Well, that I'm a queer, for instance.'

He put down his paintbrush and his eyes glittered as he stared through me. 'Well, we know you are. So what else is there to say?'

'How do you know I am?' I tried to sound calm.

'Didn't you tell everyone the night you were admitted?' I nearly fainted. 'Roaring and bawling, you were, when the nurses tried to undress you. "They're locking me up because I'm a queer." That's what ye were shouting.'

'But I'm not,' I said. He kept staring at me, and I had to look away, to observe the bedlam around us.

'In here,' he said thoughtfully, 'there are no fucking surprises left. You can be queer, black, yellow, one-legged, even an Orangeman like Franz Josef, and nobody gives a curse. Madness, old fruit, is the great leveller.'

He squeezed my arm with bony fingers and suggested

we go for a walk in the grounds.

'He thinks he's smarter than everyone,' Fred said when he spotted Roger sitting on the grass reading a book. Roger was a student from Rathfarnham. He had opted out of second-year Arts in Trinity, but he never talked much about his background. There was nothing there that could not be dismissed with a bored shrug. We tended to sit together at the therapy sessions and watch, with amused detachment, the histrionics of the others. But Fred didn't like him. I suspected that the aversion went deeper.

Roger and I used to go to a quiz every Tuesday evening in the hospital theatre. Roger usually got all the answers right. He also seemed to know more about the ailments of the patients than the doctors, and his knowledge of pharmacy was impressive. He knew the functions and side effects of every medication and had a plausible explanation whenever a patient acted more strangely than usual. He said that Franz Josef was simply a manic depressive who would soon come out of his mania, and sure enough, a few days after his prediction, I noticed the old man in the coffee shop. He was dressed, groomed and making pleasant small talk with the waitress. It was a transformation from the wild-eyed biblical patriarch of Ward 3B.

'You imagine people are talking about you because you obviously have something to hide,' Roger said one afternoon when we were sitting in the hospital coffee shop observing the awkward body language of the visitors.

'I'm not hiding anything,' I protested.

'Of course you are. We all are,' he said, and I knew there was no point in crossing him. He was simply too bright. He wasn't afraid of anything. He knew how the hospital worked. Mental illness had no mystery for him. It was all a matter of blood levels and damaged brain cells, and he used to get irritated whenever anyone in the group tried to explain their disorders in any other context. Family, culture, background, sexuality, feelings – these were all merely a part of the problem, like damaged emotional tissue. His certainty about everything was what Fred disliked so much about Roger. Fred was all fumbling human frailty, a mass of delusions and contradictions bundled up behind a well-worn mask.

Roger looked at me across the Formica table. I noticed how weak his eyes were in the glare of the canteen. They were watery brown, insipid even. He was trying to size me up, not because he was really interested but more probably because he was bored. His passion was boredom.

'You think people are talking about you, and I suppose they are, because you are projecting your fears onto them.'

'What fears?'

'Rejection. You are afraid of them rejecting you.'

'Ah, bullshit,' I said.

But he was nearer the truth than anybody else I had spoken to about my illness. At least he didn't deny my fears, as my friends and family did. By talking this way with Roger, a lot of the panic began to dissolve. He had no moral axe to grind. He wasn't judgemental. I gave him a written version of my night in the Richmond Hospital when I thought I was dying of some horrible disease. When he had read it, he roared laughing.

'You couldn't have been so stupid,' he said, taking off his spectacles to wipe them.

'I was. I really was.'

When I told him about the gas oven and the bath and falling off the roof of St Patrick's, we both collapsed with laughter. The relief was sheer bliss. No amount of medication or Gestalt Therapy could have shifted so much shame and embarrassment as did that hysterical laughter. We were laughing so much, we infected the patients around us. For a moment, the entire canteen was in an uproar, and some of the visitors looked nervous.

7

Within a week of Fred's leaving the admission ward, Mr B. was also up and dressed and coming down to the coffee shop. He spent most afternoons there with Fred and some of the older patients, smoking and drinking mugs of tea. It was a surrogate pub. Whenever visitors complained about the cigarette smoke, the group shuffled out to the grounds, where they sat by the croquet lawn. It was a beautiful September, a golden Indian summer of warm sunshine and cool, smoky evenings, when the heavens dazzled over the sycamores in the grounds and the rooftops of the city.

One day, we were sitting around on the lawn when Aileen began to play the violin. She had been a patient for a number of years and was completely institutionalised. Her face was like that of a doll, but sometimes the spirit moved in her and we glimpsed the beautiful girl she had once been. Her conversation was usually incoherent, but when she started to play, some kind of genius burst forth from her, and notes of exquisite sweetness and sadness soared above the grounds.

Fred was enthralled. When Aileen had finished playing 'The Cualain', he jumped up, applauding furiously.

'Perfect. Perfect. You'll be top of the bill.' Then he wheeled around to Franz Josef, who was dozing off in the sunshine.

'Now, Mr Brennan, we'll have your recitation.'

Franz Josef calmly got up from his chair and walked towards the middle of the croquet lawn.

'It's not the fucking Gaiety,' Mr B. shouted.

'Don't mind him, Mr Brennan,' Fred said. 'In your own time, please.'

'"The Green Eye of the Little Yellow God",' announced Franz Josef, his voice booming. After a short pause for effect, he delivered the poem with all the passion of an old-fashioned Shakespearean actor. 'There is a yellow mountain to the north of Kathmandu,' he began, his eyes glittering and his lips trembling.

There was a hushed silence as his words boomed out across the grounds. He could not remember much of the poem, but he made up for it with his histrionics. When he had finished, he bowed with aplomb, as if indeed he was on the stage of the Gaiety. Fred jumped to his feet, applauding hysterically.

'Wonderful. Bravo,' he cheered.

'Top of the bill,' Mr B. shouted.

When I asked Mr B. what was going on, he told me that they were rehearsing a variety show which would be staged in the hospital theatre at Hallowe'en. 'Fred, as you can see, is directing. He will also be the bloody star.'

'But I thought he was leaving.'

'Leaving? Fred's here for good.'

Fred was in his element, fussing about the imaginary stage of the croquet lawn and barking orders at a group of ancient patients who burst into singing 'There's no business like show business'.

A few days later, Roger and I were sitting in the grounds when he said casually: 'I killed a man.'

The remark was so off-hand that at first the significance of it did not sink in. 'You killed someone?' I asked.

He yawned. 'Yeah. The court remanded me here for psychiatric assessment.'

'Who did you kill?'

'Oh, this old bloke who used walk past the house every day.'

I thought he was going to tell me the story, but he was preoccupied with Aileen, who was stretched out on the grass, sunbathing.

'I wonder does she get it in here?' he said.

'Why did you kill him?'

He didn't answer, and when I looked at him, I realised that he hadn't heard the question. All his concentration was on Aileen, who was lying on her belly on the hard, parched lawn. 'I'm going to fuck her,' he said. There was a chilly note of certainty in his voice. She seemed to be responding to his glances. He got up and went over to her, kneeling down beside her. She squirmed with pleasure as he massaged her back. They were oblivious to me staring at them. Then they began kissing in an ugly, mechanical way, tongues darting in and out of their mouths like two enraged serpents.

When I told Fred what Roger had told me, his reaction was an even bigger surprise. 'You call yourself a journalist?' he sneered. 'Wasn't that case all over the newspapers a few months ago?'

China could have declared war on Ireland's Eye a few months ago for all I knew. 'Why isn't he in a criminal asylum?'

Fred seemed genuinely surprised at my naivety. 'His family owns half of Dublin, that's why,' he said.

Roger a murderer? I just couldn't believe it.

'I'm telling you to keep well away from that smart-arse,' said Fred, and he scurried away, refusing to discuss the case any further.

Roger and Aileen were in the canteen later that evening. Aileen seemed quite elated. She called me over. Both of them were giddy, like two smug pranksters on the verge of hysteria. I knew they had had sex.

'Did Roger tell you how he killed my father?' she asked, teasingly.

'No. How did you do it, Roger?' I tried to sound casual, as if the whole matter was an extension of the therapy sessions.

'Like this,' he said, with chilly enthusiasm, as if he was about to demonstrate a solution to some mathematical problem. 'You see, he used go for a walk every day.'

'My father,' Aileen interrupted.

'It wasn't your fucking father,' Roger said. Aileen sulked and said, 'Well, I like to think it was.'

'He used walk the Grange Road,' Roger continued, 'always passing my window at the same time. I was watching something on telly. I just got up and went out to him with the poker and smashed him over the head.'

'Why?'

Aileen let out a shrill laugh. 'He did it for me,' she said.

'Why?' said Roger, contemptuously. 'Because he was there, wasn't he?'

'He's going to plead extenuating circumstances on the grounds of life-long abuse,' Aileen said. 'All fathers are fucking abusers.'

I asked him if he had known the old man.

'No, except he walked past the house every day,' Roger said, convinced that that was an adequate explanation. I didn't know what to think. The fact that he was apparently the sanest and most personable patient in the hospital made it impossible for me to believe that he was capable of such a callous crime. There had to be some other explanation. I continued to see Roger every day, and if ever the subject of the old man came up, he gave me a baffled shrug as if he too couldn't comprehend what he had done. He seemed so normal in every other way. Even Aileen's encouragement of him, because of her pathological hatred of her father, seemed normal too in this environment. I found myself exaggerating my own melodramatic story when I was in their company. I wanted to impress them, to fit into their dark world.

Aileen occasionally escaped from the hospital and was often found wandering along Benburb Street with the other prostitutes who worked in that notorious red-light area. She was always being tested for sexual diseases, and she boasted about this a lot. If she hadn't murdered her father, she certainly wanted to do so, and she gave her body to Roger gratefully, because she believed that he had done the deed for her. Her transference from musicianship to madness was extreme: one minute she was calm and sweet and making beautiful music with her violin; the next she was murderously angry.

Yet I opened up to these people and let them in on my deepest fears. I think they understood me.

It was Roger who gave me another vital clue as to how I could survive in this place when he suggested that I should defy my delusions.

'How?' I asked him.

'Yield to them,' he said. 'Become part of them. That way, you'll either sink or swim. Otherwise, by fighting them, you'll become permanently mad.'

He took part in the rehearsals for the variety show. Fred was disgusted, but the rest of the patients thought Roger deserved his moment in the limelight. He recited a poem by Baudelaire, from *Les Fleurs du Mal*, and everyone was mystified by it.

One day, his parents came in to see him. They were an elderly, respectable couple, and they huddled about their son with the frightened expressions of people whose lives had been devastated. Roger started to shout at them. A nurse hurried into the television lounge to restore peace. When I saw the hate in Roger's face, I immediately thought of the old man on the Grange Road.

'What's wrong?' I asked him after his parents had gathered their bits and pieces and scurried out.

'I told them not to come in. I told them,' he stammered in rage.

'But they're your parents!'

'I know they're my fucking parents, but I told them to leave me alone.' He stormed off to his room, his eyes dilated and red like those of the seagulls that swooped down at breakfast-time.

I was forgetting about life outside in the real world. The problems of the *Press* now seemed to belong on a different planet. I was becoming institutionalised, sinking into the routine of the hospital and enjoying the sensation of escape. I thought that I could live there quite happily. The nurses pampered me. The food was good. There were group sessions and art classes to attend, and the company was always lively and interesting. And then there was the companionship. It was like being at the boarding school that I had never gone to: days filled with adventures and journeys into strange mental climes, nights filled with escapist laughter. Above all, there was sanctuary. Why should I swap this for the unknown terrors of the outside – the drinking bouts, the guilt, the dread of exposure? Or for the unpleasantness of the *Press*, with its perpetual squabbling in an atmosphere of distrust and betrayal?

No, I would stay in there until I was better, quite happy with the possibility that I would never get better at all. I had a room in the recovery ward, which I liked. It had a monastic feel to it, with a single bed, sparse furniture and a high window looking out over the hospital grounds. Waking up in the morning felt like being back in some idealised childhood. The ward itself was like an elegant Georgian gallery, and it was decorated with magnificent pieces of Queen Anne furniture, which the cleaning ladies polished every morning. Fred said that Dean Swift haunted this ward. I liked to believe that his enlightened spirit hovered outside my room at night, keeping a sceptical watch on his house of dreams. In the corridor was a clock, which occasionally chimed. That soft music set the tone. Time stood still until it suddenly rattled and chimed like an old man's memory. Yes, I could drift back to idylls, to a purity that preceded grief and shame.

One afternoon, while I was writing a newspaper

article in my room, Roger dropped in. 'Don't mind me,' he said as he sprawled on my bed, watching as I tried to continue writing. 'What are you doing?' he asked.

'Nothing much.' I wanted him to leave, yet I was struck by his complete indifference to another person's privacy.

'I'm working,' I then said, wondering would he take the hint.

'Oh.'

After a few moments, I began to find his company unnerving and could not concentrate on what I was writing.

'What were you thinking about, when you attacked the old man?'

'I suppose I thought he was the devil.'

I didn't believe him. Roger didn't believe in devils or gods.

'The funny thing is,' he said, 'I really don't remember thinking anything at all. I remember thinking afterwards that he had a funny expression on his face as he lay there on the road. But doing it? No, I don't remember. I suppose I must have been angry. Anger is visceral – a physical thing of the blood. There's a rush of blood and you strike.'

'Was there pleasure in it?'

'Yeah.' He was a little hesitant. I wondered was he experiencing some tinge of remorse?

'What does your solicitor think?'

'Oh, insanity plea. Central Mental Asylum for a year or two. Then I appeal when I can prove I'm sane again.'

The atmosphere in the room was oppressive. Not only was the room too small for two people, but the conversation seemed to violate the kind of spirits I wanted to invoke in this sanctuary.

'What do you want?' I finally asked him.

'Why, do you think I want something from you?'

'I don't know. Do you?'

He turned around and there was a strange, weary grin on his face. 'I might,' he said. Then he stretched his body on my bed and sighed with pleasure.

'You and Aileen are the only people here who understand that madness is about choice,' he said. 'Aileen is not mad. Neither are you. Yet you both choose to be. Why?'

'Freedom to do what we like, unconstrained by any moral scruples,' I said.

'Exactly. You see, we three live in a moral limbo.' I wanted to protest but I let him continue. 'Aileen screws everyone in sight as an act of vengeance. I kill an old man because his presence annoys me. As for you' – I tensed up, wondering what he was going to come out with – 'you want to destroy yourself because you are resisting your own natural inclination to amorality. You can't live with who you are, so you must destroy yourself.'

He stretched and broke wind. He was quite handsome, despite the greasy black hair and untidy clothes. His features were refined, hinting of Protestant stock, and he behaved with an arrogance that seemed entirely natural.

'Did you ever want to kill someone else?' I asked him, half-dreading the answer.

But he turned the question round again. 'Did you never want to kill anyone?'

The door was pushed in. It was Paddy, one of the senior nurses on the ward. He glowered at Roger, lying on the bed. 'No visiting the rooms.'

Roger jumped off the bed and swept out of the room like a petulant child.

'Is everything all right?'

'Yes,' I said.

'Are you sure?'

'Yes.'

It was the first indication that the staff were keeping a discreet eye on Roger. Could he do it again? Fred had no doubt about it. 'Of course he could. He's a maniac, and he's leading you a merry dance.' We were in the pantry off the ward, and Fred was buttering a slice of toast.

'What do you mean, Fred?'

'He's getting too familiar with you,' he said, and I thought I discerned a note of jealousy.

'So?'

'So be careful.'

'But Roger is too bright to do anything in here. It would jeopardise his chances of ever getting out again.'

Fred munched the toast, making as much noise as an animal crunching a crab. 'Did it never occur to you that the fellow is a nutter and could snap at any time?'

That did not seem like the Roger I knew. There was danger around him, and it both repelled and fascinated me.

One whole wall of Fred's room was festooned with posters of Marilyn Monroe, Charlie Chaplin, Buster Keaton and Joan Crawford. Pinned onto these were humbler totems, yellowed and ancient photographs from variety shows in which Fred and Mr B. featured. One photo was of Fred as a debonaire young man in evening dress. The young lady linking him was Maggie, plump as a mermaid and with a huge mane of blonde hair. There was a kind of haunted innocence in their eyes; they seemed to roar their raw youth to the street photographer. The

Metropole was in the background, and a man in a long grey coat was scurrying past, an embarrassed smirk on his face.

Fred's room was like a dressing room in a theatre, cluttered, smelling of vague, exotic scents. Obviously the hospital authorities had turned a blind eye to his foibles.

'Did you and Maggie have an affair?'

'Yes, in a way,' he sighed.

'But none of it ever came to anything.'

He was watching me looking at the photograph. What was it all about, really? Two gay men hiding behind a vulnerable woman? That seemed too tidy an explanation. It had to have been more complex than that. A brother, a sister, a lover. Whose lover? And behind such a dense ménage à trois, what terrible insecurities and unreal expectations, what divided loyalties and unspeakable grief? These three seemed locked forever in the same Pandora's box. Whenever the subject of Maggie came up, all Fred's gaiety vanished. His face, indeed his entire body, seemed to collapse as if some malevolence from the past was sucking the life out of him.

Fred talked me into writing a sketch for himself and Mr B. for their variety show. I spent most evenings now at rehearsals. The sketch was about two drag queens who put themselves forward for election on a Fianna Fáil ticket. I thought it was funny, but Fred was cautious about anything political, afraid of offending the hospital authorities. When we rehearsed the sketch, both he and Mr B. seemed very nervous, and it fell flat.

Suddenly, Fred stopped midway and called over to the social therapist, Mrs Dunne, who was at the piano to play

'Buttons and Bows'. As soon as she started playing the old song, the two stars were immediately transformed. They were already dressed in their drag costumes – outrageously camp gowns which some of the patients in the needlework class had made for them. They began singing and clowning. It wasn't just funny, it had genuine pathos as they cracked their antiquated jokes and minced through their arthritic routines like two Archie Rice characters in *The Entertainer*.

'I say, I say, I say'ay,' began Mr B., his face contorted with lavatorial double entendres. 'My doctor says I've wind.'

'Wind?' whined Fred, registering comic dismay.

The other patients started to whistle and cheer.

'Yes, wind, wind,' Mr B. repeated.

'What did he give you for it?'

Mr B. looked down at the rest of us, a dirty grin slowly spreading across his face. He was milking this for all it was worth. 'An Aspro.'

'But that's for a headache.'

'I know.' There was a slight pause as Mr B. gathered himself for the punchline. 'But my doctor wouldn't know his arse from his elbow.'

Fred and Mr B. revelled in this old-time pantomime. Suddenly they were sharp and funny, delivering punchlines and ad libs with perfect timing. Their faces took on that vaguely sinister aspect of the music hall and, for a few moments, they were back there in their heyday. Watching them perform was delightful, yet there was a real sense of sadness in that fleeting image of their lively past.

The variety show itself was a revelation. Fred's lighting

and choreography revealed an old pro at work, and though the individual acts might have been awkward, the production was a sensation, considering that it was an amateur show by patients in a psychiatric hospital. The theatre was packed with patients, a few nervous-looking visitors, and hospital staff. Maggie came along, all tarted up. Ensconsed in the front row, she was obviously in great form, looking about her and exchanging greetings like a grande dame at an opening night.

Aileen's recital of 'The Cualain' was very moving. She had been a student at the Royal College of Music but had had to abandon her studies when she got ill seven years earlier. Now, bit by bit, she was losing everything: her personality, her teeth, her good looks. Only the raw talent remained unblemished. The audience sensed this, and they rose and cheered when she had finished. Aileen curtsied like a child and a rare, beautiful smile escaped from her. She floated off-stage. I could see Roger waiting for her.

Franz Josef appeared, startled, in the spotlight. His gritted teeth and white make-up made him look like Boris Karloff in *Frankenstein*. As he looked helplessly around the hall, I realised that he had forgotten his poem. Fred prompted him from backstage: 'There is a yella mountain, ye bloody thick.'

The audience laughed and Franz Josef took umbrage. '"The Green Eye of the Little Yellow God",' he announced solemnly. He recited the poem perfectly – at least until the last few lines, when he stopped and said: 'And that's all there is.'

When Fred and Mr B. came onstage, they were greeted with a roar. Both stars beamed with delight and then milked the audience like the old troupers that they were. Wet-brained though they might have been, something vital of their old selves remained. When their routine had finished, Fred threw kisses to his cheering fans. He looked like Gloria Swanson in *Sunset Boulevard* – the same rictus grin and desperate need in his eyes. Mr B. winked lasciviously and poked Fred's behind with his thumb. Fred shrieked, and the lights went down as he chased his partner off the stage.

Maggie seemed to be in good form. Watching her with Fred and Mr B. after the concert, it was easy to see them as they had been in their heyday: three innocents at large in the bright lights of a town that was recovering, defiantly, from the grim war years. In her good-natured mockery of Fred, there was a hint of some deep regard from the past. They seemed like two old lovers at a tentative reunion.

Later on, I saw Mr B. escorting her out to the front of the hospital. She was a little unsteady, as if she had been drinking before the show. When they got to the front door, she collapsed in tears.

'I am sorry, Maggie,' said Mr B.

'I know,' she sobbed.

I hurried away. I couldn't eavesdrop any longer on something that seemed so private and sad.

8

Adrian McLoughlin came in one evening weighed down by his new manuscript: about fifteen hundred pages of densely typed prose. I was trapped. I knew he would keep visiting me until I had read his text. 'This is my future,' he said proudly. Already people were thinking the un-thinkable: the *Press* had no future. It was bound to close down sooner rather than later because it was losing so much money in trade disputes and declining sales. I looked apprehensively at Adrian's 'future' and promised to read it for him. His 'English publisher' wanted a new draft – which seemed somewhat odd.

At first I read a few pages every day, but they were so densely packed with detail that it became almost impos-sible to assimilate. Ostensibly, the book was a thriller, but Adrian's life was writ large in the subtext, every minor de-tail of his existence faithfully recorded. It was a monu-ment. I gave a section of it to Roger to read. A day or two later, I was reading in the hospital library when Roger rushed in, full of excitement. 'That book your friend is writing, is brilliant,' he said.

'What's brilliant about it?'

'The guy is really exposing his soul. He's tortured by

women, icons, breasts, sex everywhere. It's a misogynist's bible.'

That seemed to ring true all right. Adrian's women were all stereotypes, inflated to fantasy proportions like page-three pin-ups. He adored Marilyn Monroe, Jayne Mansfield and Raquel Welch, but he was suspicious of the new generation of women journalists. He was fairly typical of his generation of forty-somethings who manned the subs desk of the *Press* and made up sexist headlines with the malicious glee of schoolboys.

Roger indicated one chapter where the main character, Carmel Flynn, attends a conference in Greece with a group of male colleagues and is swept off her feet by a handsome Greek diplomat.

'This is unbelievable. It's as strong as Hitchcock sticking the knife into Janet Leigh in *Psycho*,' said Roger.

'But how can this sort of thing excite you?'

'Because it's all so true. All men think this way, but few put it as brutally and honestly as your friend.'

I began to think again about Adrian. Was his book a product of a misogynistic system, or a clever subversion of it? I had my doubts. You work beside people for years, so you know how they think. Or do you? Maybe Adrian's life was as much a masquerade as my own. I asked Roger did he think this way about women.

He turned the question round, as was his habit. 'Why, do you think I do?'

'I don't know,' I said.

'I like fucking them.'

'All women?'

'Yeah,' he leered. 'All women – uglies, oldies, dogs, Mother Teresas.'

'Your mother?'

'Especially her.'

I had learned not to read too much into Roger's words. 'They're the ultimate sins, rape and matricide.'

He chuckled. 'Yeah.' It did seem to have some appeal for him.

Roger's home was a neat, pebble-dashed house on the Grange Road in Rathfarnham, in the foothills of the Dublin Mountains. His mother tended the garden, and the potted geraniums in the porch, and his father did the *Irish Times* crossword every day. They were both middle-aged when Roger came along.

He told his story to the group one day. He spoke in a dull monotone and shrugged a lot as he tried to describe what he thought was an average life. It was a story with its pain and passion neatly edited out. When the group began to probe, as was usual in these sessions, Roger vanished before us, leaving only a strange, smiling impression, like that of the Cheshire Cat.

But from my conversations with him, I had a fair idea of the bits he had left out. His middle-class Dublin background was not unlike my own: the same maiden aunts and musical evenings, the same petit-bourgeois notions of respectability.

'Nobody writes about the Dublin middle classes. They are a forgotten species,' he announced when we were in the coffee shop after the group therapy session.

'James Joyce did,' I countered.

He suddenly turned angry. 'Ah, he's dead. But Irish literature ever since is a celebration of either the rural gobshite or the city knacker. There's nothing in between, where most of us live.'

He stabbed a piece of cheesecake with his fork.

If his typical middle-class background was so empty and dull, why blame writers for ignoring lives like his?

He fumed. 'I resent my parents for being nice, for being so fucking civilised, for not standing up to the brutes who have driven them into the flowerbeds. I loathe my father for his timidity.'

'Come on, there's no difference between Protestants and Catholics any more.'

He glowered at me with furious contempt. 'You are the real hypocrite, with your so-called liberal credentials and your Catholic republican newspaper. "The truth in the news" my arse. When has the *Irish Press* published the truth about what's happening to Protestants in the North and here in the South?'

I wasn't sure whether he was trying to provoke me into an argument or if his anger was genuine. I was never sure about anything with Roger. 'What more could your father have done?'

'He could have stood up to them,' he shouted.

A moment later, he settled down. 'It started off with our local church. It was *our* church,' he said. 'Then the Corporation built this naff housing estate at the back of the church. Slowly but surely the place was vandalised: windows broken, walls daubed with 'Up the IRA' graffiti, cider parties at night in the grounds. The congregation just dwindled away. People were too scared to go to church any more. Dad didn't even protest, not even to the residents' association – and he was supposed to be its bloody secretary! He let those bastards smother him because he was too nice, too fucking ecumenical to protest. That's how the rot started.' I realised that he wasn't feigning.

Another morning, Roger was being grilled by Mr Meeker when old Franz Josef came in. The therapist eyed Franz Josef as he lumbered to the back of the darkened room to find a chair. Then suddenly Meeker exploded.

'Come on, Roger, tell us the truth!'

'I *am* telling the truth.'

'You told us last week that you ran away from home,' said Meeker, still raging, apparently at Franz Josef's interruption.

'Yes.'

'Did you?'

Roger sighed with impatience. 'I ran away because I had a row with my father. That's pretty normal, isn't it?'

Roger stared balefully at Meeker, who seemed at a loss for words.

Franz Josef broke the embarrassed silence. 'I ran away to join the British army. Best thing I ever did,' the old man announced as he settled comfortably in his seat.

'We'll get to you in due course, Mr Brennan,' Meeker snapped.

But Franz Josef was not to be deterred. 'The army made a man of me. Especially Aden. There was dirty business there.'

'Mr Brennan, we are dealing with Roger today.'

Nothing upset Meeker more than a disruption of his routine. It made him tense and angry, and this in turn unsettled his patients. Roger, I saw, was delighted at the prospect of hysteria. But Meeker was being unreasonable to Franz Josef, who obviously had a lot to say.

'Do you want to tell us about Aden?' I asked him.

'I do.'

Meeker turned to Franz Josef. He was quivering with anger. 'I'm afraid, Mr Brennan, you'll have to leave unless you stay quiet.'

Franz Josef sulked for a few moments and then got up to leave. 'If I was thirty years younger, you'd be interested,' he said, and slammed the door behind him.

Roger laughed first and then the others joined in. A triumphant smirk crept across Meeker's face. I excused myself and left. It was only a small protest, but I felt that it was necessary.

I found Franz Josef sitting in the corridor being comforted by Fred.

'What did I tell you?' said Fred. 'That Meeker fellow is a fraud. He knows as much about therapy as would fill a bishop's tight little hole.'

Franz Josef nodded gravely.

Fred took the old man by the hand and the pair went off towards the canteen.

I eventually read Adrian's typescript. It was, as Roger said, a marvellous achievement. The depth and range of its misogyny was quite startling. Here, writ large, was the subliminal tabloid sexual disgust of the *Press*: women as whores or icons, men as Hollywood stereotypes, James Deans and John Waynes. But there was something desperate in the meticulous detail about Dublin architecture and street life: pages and pages of irrelevancies about Georgian characters and incidents. What was Lord Norbury, 'the hanging judge', doing in a modern romantic thriller?

I thought it would never get published. It seemed at once too oppressively personal and too disparate, a painstakingly detailed family epic that could be of interest only to a very small number of people. I wondered if Adrian had invented the English publisher.

9

Adrian came in one night in early November. I had dreaded this visit. How was I to tell him that I thought his book was unpublishable? But strangely, he didn't even ask me about it. He was already in the grip of a new passion: model trains. This was, of course, typical of Adrian, whose life was a series of obsessions. He had with him a model of the *Orient Express*, and said that he was constructing a model train system in his new lodgings in Drumcondra. As he described his plan – a room with mountains, telegraph poles, viaducts, tiny model towns and toy trains spinning up walls and across floors – I realised that he was wholly absorbed with this new adventure. The book was forgotten.

A week later, John J. Dunne came to visit. It was a mild afternoon, and we sat in the grounds. He wanted to know about the ghost of Dean Swift who haunted the hospital. John was writing a book called *Haunted Ireland* at the time. He was very nervous of the patients who were wandering about. I noticed a long-stay patient, nicknamed Bridie Butt, watching us. Bridie spent all her waking hours cadging cigarettes from patients and visitors. She fixed her eye determinedly on John. I sensed him stiffen. Bridie approached and said to him: 'Have ye gotta fag?' John jumped up and fled, his ears flattened back like a hare escaping from a fox. When I caught up with him in the car park, I tried to reassure him that Bridie was harmless.

'Harmless?' he yelled. 'She looks like Lizzie fucking Borden' – and off he went in pursuit of other ghosts.

Bridie Butt spent most of her time in the canteen or at the front entrance. As soon as an unsuspecting visitor opened a packet of cigarettes, she pounced with predatory intent. 'Have ye gotta fag' was all she ever said. By now she had spent a lifetime in the hospital. Years before, she used to carry a teddy bear around with her. She called it her baby, Monica. But the teddy bear disappeared, and Bridie, as she sagged into age and obesity, forgot her mothering instincts. Fred said that her family had dumped her in the hospital when she was a young girl. Bridie had had a baby, which she had been forced to give up for adoption. Apparently her family were rich but they had stopped visiting her years ago.

At this stage of my recovery, I was permitted to leave the hospital for a few hours at weekends. Once, I went into town with Roger. Outside the hospital, his company was strange and unsettling. As we sat in Bewley's Café in Grafton Street, I saw what I had not seen before: Roger was different. He had the grey-green pallor of madness; his anger and sullenness were becoming tiresome; his self-absorption drained the energy out of the day; and trying to hold a normal conversation with him in the café was an exhausting experience. I sat, smoking incessantly and listened to his whingeing. At one level, his rage was understandable: disappointment in his parents may have been a symptom of something much deeper, a kind of spiritual despair at the loss of cultural identity. Catholic Ireland was not a safe haven for Protestants. Then, out of his confused and angry conversation, came that old man again, the one he had killed. 'He used pass our house every day, this smirking little runt striding off to morning Mass.'

'You killed him because he was a Catholic?'

Roger ignored my question. He was back on the Grange Road in Rathfarnham. He seemed suddenly frightened, as he glimpsed the enormity of his deed. 'The exact same time, every day! He always seemed to grin passing our house, fondling those fucking Rosary beads. I just ran out and hit him across the head. It seemed to be the most natural thing to do. He looked at me like an animal and squealed. I hit him a few times, and when he fell on the footpath, I kicked his bald little head as if it was an egg.'

He took a cigarette from my packet and lit it. 'People don't kill someone just for walking past their house,' I said.

'They do. In Northern Ireland they do it all the time. But here, when you do it, they think you must be mad. You have to be mad to kill some harmless old Catholic walking down the road.'

I didn't believe him. I think he had constructed the whole fantasy about Protestant victimisation in order to conceal a story which was smaller, more private and intense, and probably about his father.

How could I have believed otherwise – that there might have been a germ of truth in Roger's story about political betrayal and social exclusion? This was 1976, after all, and we were living in the kindest and most enlightened republic in the world; a republic aglow with the democratic ideals of Wolfe Tone and the Protestant United Irishmen. Roger was the one who was deluded. Certainly not us, children of de Valera's crazy dreams. The fact that the IRA was gleefully murdering Protestants in our name simply did not register with me.

Adrian's kind of madness was altogether different. It was rooted not in chemistry but in time and place, in a kind of desperate hope. We were alike in many ways. His book and model trains mirrored my own surreal, alcoholic adventures.

When I called to his new apartment in Drumcondra, his landlady was in the front room watching television. At first she ignored me, but when I continued ringing the bell, she hobbled out, cursing. Just as she opened the door, there was suddenly a great commotion overhead, as something rattled across the ceiling and shook the entire house. She looked up in despair. 'Jesus Christ,' she wailed, 'it's the *Orient Express* again.'

Adrian was on his knees in the middle of the room, mesmerised like a small boy, as model trains spun and rattled around him. They were running up walls, across papier-mâché mountains and under makeshift tunnels. There were miniature towns and cities along the tracks, and I could make out Vienna, Paris and Budapest. The same meticulous detail that went into his book was also here. He must have spent months researching this, and then painstakingly putting it all together. I never asked him the obvious question: what was it really all about? Instead, I stepped right into his fantasy, and we sat on the floor together, discussing the myriad little touches required to coordinate the number of trains whizzing across a giant set of Europe. His pride and joy was obviously the *Orient Express*. It started at Ostend under the kitchen sink, rattled across France, which he had situated on top of the kitchen presses, down central Europe, and over the floor to some beanbags, which he had labelled 'Carpathians'.

He switched off the system and turned to another obsession of his at that time: the decline of the *Press*. I could feel myself switching off. I wanted to go back on the fantasy trip across Europe, to anywhere but Burgh Quay. Although the *Press* was my livelihood, I had lost all interest in the place.

'What would you do if the *Press* closed?' Adrian asked me.

'Get a job on another paper, I suppose.'

'No other paper would touch you with a bargepole with your record,' he said.

I knew he was right but I didn't care. I was due back in the *Press* before Christmas but I couldn't bring myself to think about it. All I wanted was escape – to get on the *Orient Express* and travel to a new world.

'You're on your last chance,' he warned me.

'So?'

Adrian looked at me wearily and shook his head. I always felt that I was on my last chance. I hoped that the *Press* would finally close down while I was in hospital, so that I would be spared the ordeal of returning to the scene of so much turmoil.

When I got back to St Patrick's, the hospital seemed deserted. Many of the recovery-ward patients were still out for the day. It was a mild, dry evening after a day of sunshine. They call this 'St Michael's Little Summer', those

few days of unseasonal sunshine in November when nature has a quiet breathing space before the full onslaught
of winter. I went out to sit in the grounds, near the chapel.
I was beginning to feel at peace with myself at last. My
'madness' seemed to have gone. I did get the occasional
panic attack, and with it all the imagined terrors of a police investigation and a public trial. But the hospital was a
real sanctuary. The staff were kind and loving, I had
things to do, and I had company in the evenings. I imagined that college could have been like this – Castleknock,
maybe, where I had dreamed of going as a child.

The chaplain came out of the chapel. He was an
elderly man but with a boyish sense of humour. 'You're
looking much better. It takes time, you know.'

Then he patted my hand and asked me did I want confession. I was taken aback by this because I hadn't gone
to confession in years. Where should I start? The chaplain
seemed to know my thoughts because he chuckled and
said: 'Let's not be so formal. Maybe you'd just like to chat
about it?'

I decided I would start with the incident at the dog
pond in the Phoenix Park, and tell the whole story from
that point. He listened patiently, occasionally sighing in
recognition as I described the suicide attempts and panic-
driven adventures into the alcoholic world of early-morning pubs. He must have heard this sort of thing every day.
When I had finished my story, he turned to me and said:
'Every road we take has a purpose. You don't know, as
yet, what your purpose is, but in due course it will become
clear to you. You've been through hell and back, and now
you're here trying to make sense of it all. You will. In time,

you will. You must have patience. Remember, *festina lente.*'
Then, patting me on the hand again, he got up. 'And another thing,' he said, walking away. 'Think how lucky you are compared to so many in here who have lost all sense and hope.'

I was more excited and relieved by this than by all the bland and cheerful pep talks from the therapists and doctors. He hadn't shown disgust at my story. The relief this gave me was so powerful that for a few moments I was hysterical, whooping with delight as if I had won a million pounds. 'I am not dirty!' I heard myself shouting into the darkening evening.

After tea, I called on Fred to tell him what the priest had said. There was no one else around to share my excitement. I also felt that Fred had a better idea of what I had gone through than anyone else. But he didn't seem impressed.

'Sure, that old sky pilot tells all the headcases that they're better,' he said. 'He'd have them all, Roger, Mr B., Aileen, even Franz Josef, out those gates in no time.'

But I couldn't be deflated by Fred's scorn. I knew he didn't want me to leave. He would have tried anything to get me to stay on in the hospital, even persuading me that I was incurably mad, like himself. He was sitting at his table scribbling on a jotter.

'What are you doing,' I asked.

'I'm writing to the Minister for Health, that's what. I'm making a formal complaint about the conditions in here.'

He threw his pen across the room in temper. 'They won't let me out for a walk unless a nurse brings me. It's fucking ridiculous.'

Then he looked at me and asked: 'Do you think I'm dangerous?'

'No, of course not.'

'But they do,' he wailed.

I had heard the rumours around the hospital that he was forgetful, that he could stray off and be a danger to himself and to others. But I couldn't see Fred as a threat. He was a kind, caring, hurt old man. Maybe the threat lay in the perception of him as a homosexual? Maybe the years inside the institution had demonised him in the eyes of the staff? Homosexuals were supposed to be dirty old men, molesters of children. That's what people believed.

'Why are they keeping you under observation, Fred?'

'I don't know,' he said with a haunted look in his eyes.

As I was leaving, he said: 'If I tell ye something, promise you won't breathe a word of it to anyone.'

'I promise.'

'Meself and Mr B.,' he whispered 'are planning to escape from here.'

10

Pop came in most afternoons, and on sunny days we sat out in the grounds watching the strange hospital world drift by. He never complained about these visits. I felt that he rather liked coming in: the alternative was sitting at home, alone. I never asked him what it was like to have a son in a lunatic asylum. I'm sure it must have been distressing, but he hid it very well, always displaying a calm, philosophical acceptance of the situation. Even in the midst of bedlam, he was forever gently tugging me back to reality: the problems of hospital bills, the *Press*, my need for toiletries and clean clothes. I never dreamed that he would die before I could work out with him all the unresolved tensions of our relationship. No, madness prevented such fears. Pop was just always around: the solid, silent centre of my troubled world.

One afternoon he appeared, as usual, carrying a plastic shopping bag containing clean underwear, socks and a new toothbrush. He looked tired after the walk up the steep hill from Parkgate Street. We sat in the elegant front hall of the hospital, where the consultants had their rooms. Suddenly he looked up at me with a slightly abashed smile, and for the briefest moment I saw an old man's fear in his eyes. What was the matter? I asked him, but he only shrugged. He would never unburden his troubles. Fathers were supposed to be strong and reserved.

'I walked down through the Buildings,' he said, changing the subject. He could easily have said that he had bought a new packet of J-cloths, or that he had mown the front lawn. Our conversations were peppered with mundane domestic details. The Buildings he talked about was an area of red-bricked, terrace streets that was also known as Oxmantown. It was one of the oldest parts of the city, and Pop took pride in its rich history. When he said that he had walked through the Buildings, I imagined that he was thinking of the ancient Norse settlement there and the woodland which had provided timber for Westminster Abbey in the Early Middle Ages.

'Why did you come the long way?' I asked him.

'Oh, I just needed the walk.'

Then he said: 'I saw winos, some younger than you, hanging about in Brunswick Street.' I knew that at the back of his mind was the fear that I would end up on skid row.

My doctor had no doubts about my illness. It was alcoholism, pure and simple. The delusions were a product of drink and nothing else. I could go home with a clean bill of health. Dr Dempsey was a big, red-faced countryman who seemed too distracted by the administrative business of the hospital to be really concerned with the mental state of its patients. He was irritated when I began to question him about my delusions.

'Ah look,' he finally bellowed across his untidy desk, 'just take the Antabuse and leave all that mind stuff alone.'

He wasn't the type of psychiatrist with whom one could discuss sexual problems. When I hinted at sex, he glowered over at me and grunted impatiently: this was more of that infernal 'mind stuff' which made his job so difficult. I could see why Mr B. was terrified of him. Dempsey was one of the more colourful sights in the hospital as he charged like a bull around the wards, waving sheaves of paper while nurses and juniors flapped along beside him. He seemed to have powers of life and death over patients like Mr B. and Fred, whom Dempsey regarded as incorrigible old lags.

I spent three minutes in his cramped little office – during which time the phone rang incessantly – and he was ushering me to the door before I could ask him any further questions. 'Yeah, yeah,' he kept saying with mounting impatience.

Outside, I saw Mr B. coming down the corridor. 'Well, is he letting you home?' he asked me.

'He didn't say.'

Mr B. mused over this. 'Did you ask him any questions?'

'I tried.'

'He doesn't like questions. That's a sign of stress, he says. He'll probably keep you in till Christmas.' Mr B. was deadly serious. I had heard too many stories about Dempsey's arbitrary decisions. He had sent patients back to bed rest (and months of incarceration in the admission ward) simply for crossing him in some minor way.

'I'm sure Fred must have given him cheek and that's why they've put him down in the loopy ward,' Mr B. said.

'I hear you and Fred are planning to escape,' I said.

Mr B. was surprised. 'Fred has a mouth bigger than a priest's arse.'

'But how – there's no way out of here.'

'Oh, we'll find a way,' he said, loping off down the corridor.

A week after that, I was to receive the full force of Dempsey's temper when I had my first relapse since the treatment began. It happened after I had secured a pass to go into town for the morning. It was only 10.30 AM and I was walking down through the market stalls of Thomas Street when I passed a pub and got that first intoxicating smell of drink. I was overpowered. It was a filthy, dark old cavern of a pub, and the only other customer was an ancient, shawled crone bent over a pint of Guinness. She was obviously a street trader. I ordered a large vodka, my hands shaking like someone with the palsy.

'Are ye all right, son?' I jabbered some excuse about being in hospital the night before.

'Oh. St James's?'

'No. The other one.'

She gulped down her drink and wiped a smear of froth from her mouth. 'Ah, ye shouldn't have gone in there, son,' she said. 'Sure that's a lunatic asylum.' She turned to the barman. 'They have alcoholics and all in there! Don't they, Tommy?'

Tommy didn't raise his head from the sink, but I could see from his grave expression that he fully concurred with the old woman's remarks. 'What took ye in there, son?'

I was so desperate for a drink that I ignored her.

When the barman served me another vodka, I heard her muttering: 'Well, ye wouldn't find me in a place like that anyways.' I drank the vodka slowly, relishing every delicious drop of it, and then I ordered another. 'Your health,' the old woman said, raising her glass and eyeing me suspiciously. 'Cheers.'

I didn't know how the hospital staff found out that I had taken drink, because I tried to conceal it when I got back, avoiding direct contact with the nurses and staying in my room for the rest of the evening. The next morning, however, Dempsey arrived before breakfast. He stood at the door and roared: 'You were drinking yesterday.'

I remembered Mr B.'s advice about not contradicting him.

'If you ever come back to this hospital again with drink on you, I'll have you sent to Grangegorman.'

When he made that particular threat, I lost my temper and told him that I was discharging myself. He had a silly, bovine grin on his face.

'You can't discharge yourself. We'll send the police after you.'

'Look, get me the forms to sign. I'm leaving now.'

'You would discharge yourself against medical advice?' he roared.

'Yes.'

'What about your family? What about your job? They won't take you back if you don't finish the course.'

He sat down on the bed and tried to reason with me, his bluff tone suddenly gone. But my mind was made up. I had gotten the taste of alcohol and I needed to get out for more, whatever the consequences. He cajoled and badgered me and tried every ruse to make me stay. When threats didn't work, he tried calm reasoning, but to no avail. I simply had to get out in order to get drunk. I never needed alcohol so much as I needed it then. I could see the froth on the old woman's lips and smell the sweet, tantalising aromas of the morning pub. Now that the delusions had gone and I felt better for the first time in years, the need for alcohol had become more acute. I wanted to drift around the Dublin pubs in an alcoholic stupor, and feel that wonderful, sloppy, sentimental charge that only booze could provide. I wanted to cry salty tears for the past again. Booze and the past beckoned once more, and nothing could stop me. Dempsey, Pop, the *Press*, fear, self-disgust – nothing.

Dempsey gave up and bolted out of the room. I waited an hour for him to send me the discharge papers, and then I went to enquire about the delay. The staff nurse told me that Dr Dempsey was seeing a patient. I told her that I had packed my bags and was about to leave. She seemed kind and was anxious to help. 'Have some breakfast first,' she said, ushering me towards the ward canteen. But I couldn't wait a minute longer. I thought I would die if I didn't get out immediately. My plan was to go to the same pub in Thomas Street, and have the first few drinks with the old woman. She was my contact now. We would go on a pub-crawl together, and I would delight in her sardonic Dublin humour.

The nurse told me that I couldn't leave without a signed pass. I pleaded with her to ring Dempsey. She picked up the phone, and dithered. In that split second, I looked to the entrance to see if there was anybody on security there. I was going to take my chance and run. If they did send the police after me, I would still manage to get a few drinks down. Then I saw Pop coming into the hospital. My instinct was to run and hide in the men's toilets until I could find a way out somehow. But Pop had already seen me. The game was up. He said that the hospital had rung. I could see that he was sick with worry. But nothing that he said really registered, because my mind was in such turmoil. He walked me back to my room. I went through all the motions of compliance, but I was furiously thinking of finding a way out that day, or, at the very least, some way of getting Roger to go out and buy me a bottle of vodka in an off-licence.

I don't know how long Pop stayed. It seemed hours. He sat by the bed in defeated silence, looking completely baffled. I imagined vodka trickling through my system. I could see an old wildlife film: the scene was an arid African landscape, suddenly bursting to life with the first drops of the monsoon rains. I remember thinking that if I had even a drop of alcohol, I could then talk to him, reassure him, answer his questions. The tiniest drop would have sated my ravenous thirst. There was a knock on the door, and Dr Dempsey looked in. 'Well, has your father talked sense into you yet?' Pop smiled grimly. I was already formulating another plan – my mind racing ahead of both of them. I told them that if I was to stay, I would need to get out occasionally, to attend the union meetings then taking place in Liberty Hall as a result of the dispute in the *Press*. Pop looked to Dempsey for guidance. They were both deeply suspicious. But then Dempsey relented – insisting, however, that I would have to take Antabuse before leaving the hospital. But Pop was troubled. He knew me too well. He knew that I would head straight for a pub as soon as I left, no matter how much Antabuse was given to me. I remembered what Mr B. had said about vomiting up the substance as soon as possible, in order to take alcohol without danger.

So, concessions agreed, Dempsey left the room, convinced that only a suicidal madman would drink on top of Antabuse.

'I know it's rough on you,' Pop murmured as he too got up to leave. He seemed quite emotional. It was really a last desperate plea to me to stay sober. But I was miles away, getting gloriously drunk in the pubs of Thomas Street.

As we walked back to reception, I saw Roger sitting with his luggage. There were two male nurses beside him. Just as I was about to approach him, his parents walked in the front door. The atmosphere was one of family crisis. Roger didn't acknowledge my presence. He looked completely lost, like a wartime child sitting in a railway station, awaiting evacuation. He was finally leaving for the criminal lunatic asylum in Dundrum. I felt sorry for him. Despite all the rage between himself and the old couple, they were the only ones for him now on his last journey from freedom. He had killed a man. His psychiatric assessment was now complete, and the case was closed. The system had decreed that Roger be incarcerated in Dundrum with other psychopaths, possibly for the rest of his life. I had to look away. I couldn't even wish him well.

'You should be home for Christmas,' Pop said, reassuringly, as he left.

After tea that evening, I went to look for Mr B., hoping that he might take pity on me and give me a drink from the stockpile which, I was convinced, he had hidden somewhere. It was futile. Mr B.'s secret store was his most precious possession. I should have realised that asking him for booze was like asking a famine victim to surrender his bowl of rice. He denied that he had any drink, but I could smell it on his breath.

Where did he keep it? His room didn't have any obvious hiding places. Fred hinted at a network of suppliers – former patients who came bearing gifts. Then, presumably, Mr B. poured the alcohol into Lucozade bottles, aftershave containers and even the Lourdes holy water receptacle which he kept, suspiciously, in his drawer. Occasionally, the nurses discovered his secret hiding places, but Mr B. usually managed to find somewhere else. They probably gave up on him in the end.

'How the hell would I have booze in here?' he roared at me, guilt written all over his face. 'Look around you. There's nowhere to hide it.'

'Is there no way of getting out of the hospital unnoticed,' I asked him.

Mr B. shook his head. If anybody in the hospital knew a way out, it would have been him. He must have pondered this question many times over the years: an old lag with all the time in the world to plan a great escape.

'The only way you can get out of here is through the front door – with their permission.'

'But you and Fred are planning to escape. Let me go with you,' I pleaded.

Then I saw a glint of mischief in his eyes. 'What night is this?'

'Thursday,' I replied.

'There's an AA meeting in the hospital at eight.' He studied my reaction.

'You could slip out when the AA crowd are leaving. That's providing whoever's on reception doesn't see you.'

He winked at me. 'Fred will help out. It's an old trick and it always works. You don't have to worry about a thing. Just come out of the meeting with a few of the AA heads and walk casually towards the door with them. Leave the rest to us.'

Mr B. tucked a fiver into my shirt pocket. 'Bring me back a naggin of Irish,' he said, and his face was livelier now than I had seen it in weeks.

The AA people were remarkably well-groomed and bursting with good health and confidence, which contrasted starkly with their individual stories of degradation. I felt guilty sitting among them, contemplating what I was about to do. At times I wanted to tell them what I was thinking; to come clean. But I could taste the vodka, feel the giddy sensation of drifting into unreality, and I was shaking again in anticipation. One woman seemed to address her remarks directly at me. I thought that she could somehow read my thoughts, and this made me even more agitated. 'I thought I knew all the tricks in the book,' she said. 'But what a fool I was. How can you know all the tricks when your life is going fast down the sink?' I tried not to look at her, but even with my head bowed, I could feel her warm blue eyes fixed on me. I felt dirty and shameful.

After the meeting, the group stood and recited the Lord's Prayer and then we adjourned to another room for tea and biscuits. Again, I felt the loving camaraderie between them. They were survivors from the same wreck-age. They were on first-name terms with each other. They didn't look like alcoholics. Not one of them looked like Fred or Mr B. They seemed to exude glowing, robust normality.

I walked with them out to the reception area, where there was a sudden commotion. Patients and visitors scur-ried in every direction as Fred and Mr B. started tearing into each other. So this was their distraction! Fred was hys-terical, scratching at Mr B. and screaming arcane insults, like some ancient prostitute in a lane off Benburb Street. The receptionist – a burly young male nurse – was franti-cally endeavouring to keep them apart, but still they man-aged to exchange blows. I knew that they were enjoying themselves.

'You're only a two-bit sex pervert,' Mr B. taunted.

'Yoor the fuckin' pervert, ye sodden old bastard!' Fred screamed, and he grabbed a clump of Mr B.'s hair.

'Ah lads, ah lads,' the poor nurse pleaded, and when two AA members went over to help him restore order, I saw my chance, backed away to the front door and then si-dled out into fresh air and freedom. I walked briskly down the avenue, not daring to look back. When a car stopped behind me, I was convinced the game was up, but it was only one of the AA men whom I had spoken to earlier. He offered me a lift. I thanked him but declined, explaining that I had only a few hundred yards to go. When I reached the front gate of the hospital, I felt a thrill of relief. The traffic on Thomas Street, the roar of the city, the sounds of normal people coming and going from pubs and shops, all proclaimed my freedom. I got to the little pub, my heart pounding with excitement. It was packed and noisy. A rough-looking crowd of young men eyed me suspiciously as I made my way to the bar and ordered a double vodka and a pint of lager. I didn't want to leave anything to chance, to the possibility that a squad of burly men in white coats would come crashing through the door at any moment. I would drink doubles or trebles until the initial danger had passed.

There was no sign of the old woman from the other morning. She was obviously a daytime tippler – a real professional, as Mr B. would say. Night drinkers, he often said, were only 'piss-artists and amateurs'. I drank the vodka but it had no kick. That was a disappointment. I had expected an electric surge to the head. Maybe the mood was wrong. I sought a quiet corner away from the noisy young crowd and gulped down the lager, but there was still no kick. I thought of something one of the AA members had said at the meeting: 'I used to drink myself sober. But even drink couldn't do anything for me any more.'

I had another large vodka and calmed down a little, but still there wasn't that buzz I craved. I liked that quiet corner. I felt I could disappear there, into the alcohol and the dreamy world it created. But something was wrong. Instead of sinking into blissful escape, my mind remained sharp and focused. I couldn't stop thinking about those kindly people at the AA meeting and how I had abused their trust. I had allowed them to share their wonderful new world of recovery with me, while all the time I was planning this escapade. I drained the vodka down my throat, but still nothing happened. I ordered another pint of lager and a large vodka, ignoring the startled expression on the barman's face, and when I drank this ravenously, the shakes began. This was the reverse of what I thought was the norm – alcohol was supposed to get rid of the shakes, not start them up anew. I sat in the corner, shaking and sweating, every sip inducing waves of depression and disgust. I decided to go back to the hospital. I left a half-empty pint and rushed out of the pub like a frightened animal.

When I got back to the hospital, the receptionist looked up as I walked in. His eyes narrowed, suspiciously. 'Have they cooled down yet?' I asked, feigning an air of amused indifference. He raised his eyes to heaven. Then he asked me if I had gone out. 'No, I was just walking the avenue to get some air.' I was still shaking and sweating when I got to my room. I wanted to confess, to tell Dr Dempsey, or anyone, what a terrible discovery I had made. I lay on the bed and cried with frustration. The alcoholic kick had gone, yet I still craved it. I pleaded with God to take me during the small hours, because I knew that I could not live with a craving that could not be satisfied.

Fred and Mr B. burst into the room. They were both agitated, having heard that I had come back to the hospital. When I told them what had happened, they stared blankly at me.

'What a fucking waste,' Fred muttered as he stared grimly out the tiny, barred window at the tennis courts below.

Mr B. raised his hand as if to prevent his pal from launching a tirade against me. 'Look, you didn't give yourself a chance,' Mr B. said. 'Another few scoops, and you would have been as right as rain.'

He plonked his huge body in the armchair beside my bed, emitting a volcanic sigh. 'You've been on the dry too long,' he explained patiently. 'You have to ease your way back. Sometimes it can take a day's boozing before I can get that kick.' This was one of those moments when I thought that Mr B. knew more about alcoholism than anyone else in the world – more than Dr Dempsey and the young therapists who fussed about every aspect of one's 'alcoholic behaviour' with cheery fanaticism. He looked at me with pity, and shook his head. I had obviously disappointed him greatly. 'You'll be going up the walls tomorrow for a drink, and now you've blown it. You could so easily have brought yourself back a cure.'

Fred nodded bleakly in agreement. He remained standing at the window, staring out into the night. I lay back on the bed and closed my eyes, hoping that they would leave me alone. It was unsettling: Fred's angry, twitching silence, Mr B.'s heavy breathing. They were suddenly too close. The room was too small. And then I began to suspect something else – that I had failed some kind of test.

'The one and only time I ask him to bring me in a measly naggin of Paddy, and he makes a pig's arse of it,' Mr B. snarled at Fred.

'I'm sorry,' I mumbled, not sure what I was apologising for.

Fred shrieked. He spun around from the window like some half-crazed dervish, his eyes and nostrils flaring. 'Sorry! It's our life's blood!' He was waving his long bony fingers in front of my face, and I thought he was going to slash me with his nails.

'Fred, I don't understand why you are so upset. You

didn't ask me to bring you back anything.'

'It's not that. It's not that,' he whimpered, close to tears.

'Then what is it?'

'You came back, you see,' Mr B. said.

'So I came back. So what?' I was getting irritated now.

Mr B. turned to Fred. ' "So what," he says.' Fred grinned like a dead fish, and shook his head in disbelief. We seemed to be talking in different languages.

'Nobody escapes from this place and walks back,' Mr B. fumed. 'It's just not natural.'

'What is it to you?'

'Do I have to spell it out?' Mr B. roared.

'Yes.'

I just wanted them to leave, to take their strange hurts and bizarre logic out of my life completely. Fred fluttered from the window like some huge trapped moth. 'We thought it could be done,' he said, panting. 'We thought it would be possible to escape from here and go on an almighty bender.'

'It *is* possible,' I said.

'But you walked back,' he said. 'After all the planning we did, you blew it by walking back.'

I was exhausted by this gibberish but Fred still fluttered about the room, wittering on and on. 'We spent the whole evening imagining what a great time you were having out there, getting gloriously drunk. Mr B. had a wager that you'd come back stocious in an ambulance, but I believed that once you'd tasted freedom, you'd stay away.'

Mr B. chimed in: ' "He'd be in the Ashling by now." That's what we said at about nine. We followed you through all the pubs, the Ashling, Ryan's, down the Quays to the Ormond Hotel and then into the city centre. You were sailing further and further away, and we were following you.'

Fred sat down at the end of my bed. He looked around the room desperately.

'There's no escape from here, Mr B.,' he said, with doomed resignation. Mr B. nodded glumly and looked at me as if this was my fault. His eyes were hard and cold. I felt a little frightened. I was beginning to understand why these two spent most of their lives locked away in a mental hospital. They were endeavouring to escape through me. Was I some kind of medium through whom these troubled spirits might find release?

Fred broke the uneasy silence. 'If you couldn't do it, a personable young boy like you, what chance would an old fool like me have? I would lose my nerve and run back here.' He kept staring at me. His eyes and face seemed to disappear into the Chinese patterns on his silk dressing gown. Mr B. leafed morosely through some old magazines on my bedside table. The room was full of their suffocating grief. I just didn't know what to say. I had transgressed in some incomprehensible way. Fred lit a cigarette and sucked on it.

'I am one of you,' I said feebly, but I didn't believe it, and neither did they.

Fred sneered, and cigarette smoke belched from his nostrils. He nodded to Mr B.

They shuffled towards the door, like two ancient Indians, offended by a visitor who had spurned their hospitality.

'You'll be gone in a week or two,' Fred said, opening

the door. 'You'll be out there with your new AA friends and you'll have forgotten all about us.'

Mr B. put his arm around his friend's shoulder and mumbled 'Come on' as they left the room. I lay back on the bed and tried to fathom what exactly had upset them so much. Their disappointment seemed to go deeper than the fact that I had failed them by returning, sober, to the hospital. They had latched on to me from the very beginning. I was in my twenties, and they were old men. They weaved in and out of my delusions and fears, offering friendship, even love. But what did they really want?

I was sobering up now, and getting suspicious. Did they see me as some kind of lifeline to booze, to the outside world? They behaved like men who believed that they would be in the hospital for the rest of their lives. Did they hope that I, too, would stay in their shadowy world forever?

That was it! They wanted me to stay. I was sure of it. After months of shadow and echo, I had finally made a solid discovery. I wanted to jump out of the bed and run to reveal this discovery to a counsellor or a doctor; to anyone. I had regained my sanity. They were trying to seduce me into their lost world, into their pattern of drinking surreptitiously in the hospital, defying the authorities, pining over the past, and to make me sink into the same morass as themselves. 'You'll be back,' Mr B. had said to me, the very first day I met him. He had a smug, knowing look on his face. He could see right into the dark and complex heart of things. He had seen my future and it was in there, with him and Fred, smuggling drink in for them, taking part in their pantomimes, giving them the companionship they needed and the youthful vitality they craved. I wondered was that how it was for Fred in the first place. He was a few years younger than Mr B. Had he, too, been seduced into this alternative life?

But now, Mr B. had to face the prospect that he was wrong about me, about his own certainty. Doubt was the beginning of the end, the terrifying moment before the decline into chaos. No wonder he was so disturbed.

I could have easily fallen into their trap. The lure of the hospital was sometimes irresistible to someone who wanted to escape the outside world. One could be a child again in this pristine place, a dependent human being whose every whim and desire was catered for by a mothering staff. It had the feel of a strangely recovered childhood.

Fred and Mr B. trawled the corridors, but really they lived back in the 1940s with Maggie, in the colourful world of music-hall make-believe. I knew I could have escaped into their past; gone back to a time of innocence, before sex and shame, before school and the smell of fear in the classroom. The alcoholic in me could have stepped so easily into their memory world, and lived happily ever after there.

I was still feeling queasy from the alcohol the next morning. The weather was still mild and sunny, so I sat in the grounds, beside a rockery at the back of the oldest wing of the hospital. I was surprised to see roses still in bloom, though the gardens were beginning to look straggly and autumnal. The neat order of summer had given way to swirling autumnal riot, with great mops of decaying blooms merging into each other like a half-finished

Impressionist painting. There were slugs and snails everywhere, in the rockery and across the little courtyard where I sat. The unseasonable mildness had brought them out. The milky November sunlight revealed their slimy progress. The rockery looked like a carbuncle-encrusted cliff-face at low tide. Silvery mucous trails crossed the flagstones and the pathway. Daylight seemed to stun the snails and slugs. They clung to everything – rocks, plants, the trunks of miniature trees – trapped between night and day. I sat for ages watching them, wondering if they would move back to their subterranean homes. At one stage, I thought I saw a slight movement. I thought of the old man in the Meath hospital who had spent all day trying to reach the whiskey bottle in his locker. It was a snail out on the pathway, completely exposed to every possible danger. Yet the snail didn't seem aware of the danger. I touched it; it didn't move. Other creatures would have scuttled away at the mere smell of a human, but this snail remained motionless. Maybe it was too glutted by its night of feeding to move. It could have been a drunk lying helpless in the street.

Some of the older patients were out strolling before breakfast. I noticed Aileen racing across to the chapel. She was dressed in a pink-and-white party frock, with ribbons streaming behind her as she disappeared into the chapel. Today, she was a character from *Gone With the Wind*. The seat was wet, but it didn't bother me: I was too preoccupied with the snails, the patients drifting in their daydreams, the sense of internal chaos in this apparently tranquil and sunlit scene. I walked into the rose garden, and found myself on my hands and knees trying to ascertain what other creatures inhabited this miniature jungle. There were spiders' webs everywhere – great lace curtains of them draped across the foliage. One huge brown spider hung in the centre of her web. She, too, was completely unconcerned by the dangers wheeling about overhead: a gull could have swooped down and devoured this morsel in the blink of an eye. This jungle was so completely absorbed with itself that it could not sense any danger from outside. It reminded me of the *Press*.

This place reeked of death, with everything slowly vanishing into the soil. This was the death I often dreamed about: no violence, pain or panic, just the sweetest melancholy of slipping away with Fred, Mr B., Aileen and the others. All Fred ever worried about now – apart from his daily requirement of a fix of alcohol – was the texture of his dressing gown. Did it make him too fat, he often asked me, as he sashayed in front of his bedroom mirror. Too fat for whom? I wondered. Mr B.? The other patients? He reminded me of a cat I used to see when I was going to school. It dozed in a sunlit corner of a newsagent's window in Aughrim Street. I envied that cat, her blissful indifference to the world as she dreamed about herself in the sun.

Aileen was standing over me. She seemed to have materialised out of the wilting jungle. She spoke suddenly, hysterically: 'I'm going to a new hospital today. My father said that this place doesn't suit me any more, so he's sending me to an exclusive place in the country. And it's also near the sea. That's why I'm all dressed up.' I hoped she would float back into her ward, but instead she sat down on the forecourt bench, obviously with every intention of staying. Aileen was in one of her whimsical moods: elated, wired to the moon. When she was like that, she drained energy from everyone around her.

'I hope you'll be happy there,' I said, awkwardly.

She sighed and furiously tugged at the hem of her gaudily old-fashioned dress. I was about to move off, but she raised her hand to stop me. 'I was watching you,' she said, with a hint of petulance. 'You were staring at the spiders.'

'Yes, there are so many of them, aren't there?'

'Do you think they're beautiful?' This was the first time she had ever asked me a direct question. Normally, I was on the receiving end of her self-absorbed prattle, but now she seemed aware and a little nervous.

'I suppose they are,' I said.

She thought about my answer and nodded solemnly. Then, her eyes still fixed on the rose garden, she whispered: 'My father is coming at two o'clock.'

She sounded sane. It was as if she had glimpsed her future in this 'exclusive' place in the country, and the horror of it had cleared, fleetingly, some of the mess from her mind.

'I'll see you before you go,' I lied, as I moved away towards the wards.

I wish that I had stopped a minute or two with her. I might have been able to calm whatever terrors besieged her. Now she, too, is permanently trapped in memory – a sad, broken creature trembling at the edge of her private hell.

11

I didn't see much of Fred or Mr B. during my last few weeks in the hospital. They seemed to vanish into the background – two shuffling ghosts sighted briefly in the traffic at the end of corridors. In early December, Dr Dempsey decided that it was time for me to go back to work. I dreaded the prospect of returning to the scene of so much madness. Yet it was unavoidable: the choice was between being institutionalised in the hospital system or going back to the *Press* to face the music.

The day I returned, I got up at 5.30 AM. I wanted to go in early, before anyone else, so that I would be sitting at the desk when my colleagues arrived. That would give me the upper hand. I imagined nothing more unpleasant than returning to a crowded office, with heads raised in embarrassed silence as I walked in.

As I walked down Burgh Quay early that morning, an old, familiar fear surfaced again. It was like going back to school after the long summer holidays: back to the bullying and the casual violence of the classroom. The city was astir. Dockers, coming off night shifts, drifted into the White Horse pub beside Butt Bridge. Bus conductors bought newspapers and cartons of milk in the

tiny grocery shop beside the pub. Grey-faced office workers filed out from Tara Street Station, grimacing in the
sleety east wind that whipped up from the river. I envied
these people and their normal routines.

At the back door of the *Press*, dispatch workers were
unloading rolls of newsprint from a truck. They whistled
cheerfully in the early-morning gloom. When I got to the
subs desk, only old Theo was in, and he barely noticed me.
He looked bedraggled. After a few moments, he looked
up, smiled a toothless greeting and returned to a mountain of copy, which he scratched away at. I got a whiff of
alcohol off him, and for a second I was tempted to slip out
again to the White Horse and fortify myself with a quick
vodka. A few minutes later, the editor arrived, and I was
surprised and relieved by the warmth of his greeting. He
shook my hand and said he hoped that I had fully recovered. I had disliked him intensely up to that moment – he
was a central bogeyman in my delusions, in fact – but now,
after his friendly reception, I began to relax. The poor man
had plenty of reasons for disliking me, with all the abuse
I had given him: I had often rung him at his home in the
small hours to rage at him for ruining my life.

The last occasion I rang him, just before I went into
hospital, I wanted to tell him about a scene I had witnessed
earlier that evening. It was the recovery of a man's body
from the canal in Phibsboro. In my drunken state, I had
exaggerated the story: I told him that the body was that of
the Archbishop of Dublin. The editor slammed the phone
down. Now he was patting me on the back and reassuring
me that all was right again. I thought I might have a drink
later on, to celebrate my good fortune.

One by one, the others arrived, and gradually it seemed that I was back to normal. There were no embarrassing silences or dirty looks. My colleagues were pleased to see me back. Within thirty minutes, the dread of anticipation had ceded to the dull routine of daily newspaper life. The phones started ringing, reporters raised their voices and rushed about; the momentum of the news-gathering process gathered pace. I was back to the court cases and the county-council meetings, the muggings and murders, the traumatic and the trivial. Back to the bored hum of the subs desk as my colleagues sharpened their pencils, unpacked their lunch boxes, scanned photographs, designed pages, dunked tea bags into mugs of boiling water and casually sieved morsels of news from an ever-flowing tide of human detritus. It felt as though I hadn't been away at all. It wasn't long, however, before word came down that the personnel manager wanted to see me. His secretary, a nervous, birdlike woman of about sixty, greeted me with a chilly smile. I feared the worst.

The manager was sitting back behind a large and surprisingly empty desk. 'Ah, you're back,' he said, as if he was greatly surprised. Then he leaned forward and eye-balled me. 'For good, this time, I hope?'

I noticed a tiny stain on his otherwise immaculately white breast handkerchief. As he lectured me on how difficult it was for the company to make ends meet when people like me were out on sick leave, I became fascinated by this stain. 'It hurts productivity,' he said. He seemed a little uncomfortable in my gaze. I wondered would he re-arrange his handkerchief. 'And when you hurt productivity, you hurt other people.' I sang dumb. I told myself that

I was a republican prisoner being interrogated at the infamous Castlerea Detention Centre, and concentrated on the ridiculous spot on his hanky. What I really wanted to do was to grab the slimy fellow by the lapels and shake him like a rag doll. His inept management had brought a great national newspaper to the brink of ruin. Now he seemed to be saying that my illness was the cause of all the *Press*'s woes. He warned me that any further relapses into alcoholism would result in my immediate dismissal. 'And no union would touch you with a bargepole,' he sneered.

When he had finished his lecture, I took my eyes off his hanky and did a passable imitation of Uriah Heep: reassuring him that I had learned my lesson and was deeply grateful for this second chance. He liked to see me grovel, so he sat back in his seat and allowed himself a patronising smile. 'For your own sake, try and keep it together,' he said. I got up and left, dearly wanting to swipe the smug grin off his golf-club face.

Gradually, I settled back into the routine of the *Press*. Whenever I tried to bring up the subject of my illness, there was noticeable unease at the desk, especially from John J. Dunne and Adrian, whose attitude was 'put all that behind you'. They never referred to the dramatic events which had preceded my going into hospital, and so the lid remained tightly shut on that. I still had lingering doubts: could I really have imagined everything? But it was safer not to dwell on such doubts. I knew that they would lead me back to madness.

Watkins sat beside me one day. 'You gave us all a terrible fright,' he said.

'I'm sorry about that.'

'You know,' he continued, 'you're a good writer, and you should write down all that's happened to you. It would make great reading.' I was suddenly weepy and wanted to apologise for all the animosity I had borne him over the years. 'Ring me any time if you need help,' he whispered.

I had been wrong about Watkins, about the editor, about everyone in the *Press*. My delusions had poisoned everything.

Adrian had now lost all interest in both his book and his model trains. The subject of his latest obsession was China. He was planning to visit Beijing that summer. His desk was littered with literature about the Great Wall, the Forbidden City and anything else pertaining to China he could get his hands on. So preoccupied was he with this new subject that I imagined that he was beginning actually to look Chinese. The clothes he now wore had a distinctly Mandarin style: red and yellow silk jackets and baggy trousers which he bought in the unisex boutiques in Mary Street. Whenever he went on about his admiration for Chairman Mao, Dunne would raise his eyes with a martyr's patience, and sigh. One morning, Dunne was very cranky, and I saw that he was losing his patience as Adrian twittered on relentlessly. Suddenly, through a mouth full of tomato and bread, Dunne roared: 'Why don't you fucking well stay in China if you love that old yella bollix so much!'

Dunne hated all communists. He hated the way they had broken up his romantic pre-First World War world; how they had butchered the Tsar and his family and had brought in a grey generation of socialism. He, too, lived in the past – or rather in his own idealised version of it. He pined for an age of Franz Lehar music, the silent films of Charlie Chaplin and Mary Pickford, a Dublin that was still graced by the Theatre Royal and ballroom dancing in the Metropole. He was an old-fashioned Dubliner: a staunch royalist who despised republicanism. He talked about the British royal family with a deference that bordered on madness. The *Press* was still full of old-style republicans, carried articles like 'Old IRA notes' and, editorially, re-ferred to Northern nationalists as 'our separated brethren'. While the IRA was bombing and murdering Northern Protestants, the paper adopted a chilly ambivalence to-wards the outrages – a viewpoint that reflected a sizeable section of public opinion in the South. There were no great marches in protest against the carnage, and one rarely, if ever, saw pickets on the Sinn Féin headquarters in Gardiner Street in the city centre.

Once, as John J. Dunne was editing some tired old pan-egyric to the republican dead, he tossed his biro across the desk in disgust and railed: 'Ah, Padraig Pearse – the crazy queer who led us all to freedom!' Dunne always stayed out sick on St Patrick's Day. We assumed that it was a protest against all the paddywhackery which the holiday engen-dered. But one evening over a quiet drink in his home, he mentioned that both his parents had died many years ago on this day.

Adrian and he were rival champions of some *ancien régime*. Most mornings, they sparred with each other, more in fun than in anger, but occasionally blood was drawn. Adrian was forever needling John about his favourite causes: the deposition of King Zog of Albania, or Ireland's departure from the Commonwealth. And sometimes Dunne would erupt like a lynx, spitting venom and outrage across the desk. But they always made up afterwards. They hated and loved each other in equal measure. Like Mr B. and Fred, these ageing *Press* bachelors seemed bound to each other like two survivors from a lost world.

Not long after I returned, I discovered that Adrian had almost been sacked while I was in hospital. As the film critic, he went to many receptions and film premières; these were often an excuse for a binge. One night, he attended the opening of a luxury cinema in the city centre. He arrived very drunk and made a beeline for the Taoiseach, Jack Lynch, Mairín Lynch and George Colley, who were huddled together having a drink. Adrian proceeded to urinate on Jack Lynch's shoes. There was uproar, and Adrian was ejected from the premises.

Meanwhile, the phone rang on the editor's bedside locker. 'Your film critic,' an irate cinema manager roared, 'is down here pissing all over the fucking Taoiseach!'

When I questioned Adrian about the incident, he said he had no recollection of it whatsoever. 'I must have thought I was in the loo,' he said.

Dunne refused to give me any information about the same episode. 'The less said about that, the better,' he snapped. Although the story was gleefully repeated in the pubs around Burgh Quay, it was never mentioned in the office, as the staff closed ranks and protected one of their own.

My routine then was simple and rather humdrum:

working in the *Press* during the day and returning to the strangeness of the hospital for a cold tea. This was always a slice of ham, garnished with a smudge of coleslaw, which the nurses had left for me in the canteen fridge. The evenings consisted of quiz games, concerts, lectures and discussions. The break reduced my dependence on the hospital, as Dr Dempsey knew it would, and I was never to feel completely part of St Patrick's again. In fact, my last days in the institution went by in a blur. The day I finally checked out was something of an anticlimax. A nurse handed me a prescription for the tranquiliser Librium, and asked me to clear my room. It was as impersonal as checking out of a hotel. There were no cheers or fanfares, no flowers or speeches, to wish me well on my way. I just said goodbye to the nurse, collected my suitcase, and left, without a glimpse of any of the people I had shared my life with during the previous few months. All those colourful characters had simply vanished into the institution. Fred, Mr B. and Franz Josef were probably making baskets in the day room, their minds weaving in and out of cloudy worlds.

I walked home, down the hill to Parkgate Street, where I drank so often in Ryan's pub. A group of teenage winos sat on a bench in the little park opposite the Ashling Hotel. The day was dark and drizzly and the city looked depressing. Grey faces peered out of dark anoraks; an ancient prostitute pulled on a cigarette as she huddled in a corner of Benburb Street; a string of yellow fairy lights dangled across the entrance to the hotel; wet and shivering commuters waited gloomily at a bus terminal on Infirmary Road. This was the world I had run away from – the dreary normality of a December day – and as I headed down the North Circular Road towards home, I felt a fleeting pang of regret for the warm sanctuary that I had left behind.

Pop was waiting for me. A fire was blazing in the living room, and he had roast beef cooking in the oven. 'Welcome home,' he said.

12

My recovery was a slow, tedious affair. I started to go to AA meetings at night and developed friendships with other broken people – friendships which never seemed to last. But the simple ordinariness of the basic AA philosophy – 'One day at a time' – seemed exactly right for me. As the months passed, I stopped thinking about alcohol and my adventures in the pubs of Dublin. My life became quieter and more ordered. I opened a bank account for the first time. I learned how to drive a car. I also learned to keep the lid firmly closed on that box that contained sex, delusions – in fact all the fears and anxieties that had plagued me since childhood. To stay sober, I also had to remain celibate. I didn't know it at the time, but I was a dry drunk. The more I suppressed my real feelings, the greater the trouble I stored up for the future.

I still returned occasionally to St Patrick's Hospital to attend after-care meetings. I met an elderly nun who had had her first alcoholic drink at the age of seventy-two. Within a year, she was a raving alcoholic. Another woman, a farmer's wife, used to sneak out to the pub every day. Her addiction was discovered when her husband drove past the pub and saw their chickens waiting outside: they had followed her into the town. Such stories intrigued me but I failed to get the message because I was not really serious about remaining sober. I convinced myself that a time would come when I could drink socially, like my friends and colleagues. Sometimes I spotted Fred or Mr B. They were usually in the distance – and invariably vanished, like ghosts, the moment I saw them. But after a year or two, I stopped going back.

Pop never talked about what had happened to me. He would just sigh and mumble 'Put it all behind you.' I spent a lot of time with him now, and in my quiet, humdrum recovery, I think we grew closer together. He, too, was a creature of routine – a routine which became more ordered as he drifted into old age. His day was spent getting the groceries from the supermarket, then cooking the dinner, which he always had ready when I came home from the *Press* in the afternoon. Then he dressed himself up for evening Mass in Aughrim Street church. Occasionally he visited the aunts on the Cabra Road after Mass, but he usually came home to watch television for the evening. He didn't have any male friends of his own in these last years of his life. He lived only for his family.

I heeded Watkins' advice and started writing about my experiences. At first, it was simply something to do, to keep my mind off the pub. Pop sometimes turned off the television set while I was typing, and he sat at the fire listening to the clicking of the machine. That seemed to give him great contentment. He often asked me to read out what I had written. As the stories developed, he, too, became involved with the characters. Once, I was trying to describe a character going on a date in Dublin in 1942. I asked him what his sister, Peggy, would have worn on such an occasion. He sat back in the armchair, closed his eyes, and painted a vivid picture of a shy young woman in a velour coat, a red silk dress and nylon stockings.

On these occasions, his mind often ranged back to when he was a young man during the Civil War. He described the atrocities of the Black and Tans and how they used to raid houses in the area where known republicans were holed up. Often, he would dwell on the First World War and the fate of the Dublin Fusiliers, who were all wiped out at the Somme. He knew some of those boys. He often got angry at how the Irish State had ignored their sacrifice. What he described seemed so remote, yet it was only a generation away. I would sit with him and listen, fascinated, as he talked about Passchendaele, Ypres and the Dardanelles. I would hear the traffic rumbling up the North Circular Road from town. I would hear his child's voice when he talked about his own father. He always seemed to be in awe of his father, who had died young.

Listening to Pop's stories helped me write, and remain sober. He created a mood in the old house which enabled me to trawl back into the Dublin of the 1930s and 40s, when Fred and Mr B. and Maggie were young; to trace a fictional path back to their time, so that their story became enmeshed in my own.

Slowly, a story about lost lives began to emerge and take shape. When I had finished the short story, I submitted it to David Marcus, the editor of New Irish Writing in the *Press*. As I had given him many stories, which had all been rejected, I didn't hold out much hope for this one. But Marcus surprised me. Some time later, he suggested that I turn the story into a play.

'You have very strong and colourful dialogue,' he said.

John J. Dunne wasn't surprised by this reaction. He and Adrian disliked Marcus intensely. 'Don't mind that fellow,' Dunne said. 'He's only making an excuse not to publish your story.' The thought of developing the piece into a full-length play filled me with apprehension and insecurity. Though I had reviewed many plays over the years for the *Press*, I had little confidence in my ability to write one. But the characters of Fred, Maggie and Mr B. were tugging at me, refusing to go away.

Gradually, I started back to that smoky kitchen off Ward 3B, listening again to the lost language of its inmates, taking in the smells and sounds of the early-morning tea routines, the bickering and the banter, and the sense of lost illusions that hung over the place. My father encouraged me every day. As soon as I returned home, he would say: 'Are you going to do some writing now?' I would go up to the old sitting room and sit at the window overlooking the North Circular Road. Snatches of dialogue came to me, and certain scenes began to take shape.

Within a couple of months, I had a very rough draft of the play completed. I called it *The Midnight Door*, in reference to the great door of the admission ward, which was bolted shut every night. I set the play in the kitchen off the ward on the day Maggie came to visit her brother with the news that she could not afford to pay his hospital bills any more and that he would have to be transferred to Grangegorman. But the emotional core of the play was the past – that idealised time when Maggie, Fred and Mr B. were wild and young and believed that life held great promise for them.

I gave it to Adrian to read. He liked it and suggested that I give it to Sean McCarthy, script editor of the Abbey Theatre. McCarthy had a cramped little office over the Peacock, and in those days one could just call in off the street with an unsolicited script. There were no formalities, no panels of readers, just one lone, brilliant script editor who read everything that landed on his cluttered desk.

A month later, I got a phone call from McCarthy. He said that he had read the play and would like to discuss it with me over lunch in Wynne's Hotel in Abbey Street. My heart was pounding when I arrived at the hotel. I liked McCarthy immediately. He was a large, shy man with an open, honest face and a mane of greying hair. He said that he liked *The Midnight Door* and that the Abbey would be interested in developing it. I was so excited that I couldn't eat my lunch. Sean then explained what he meant by 'development': I would have to rewrite the whole play in a more dramatically structured way. But he liked the raw power of the play and the colourful characters in it.

When I told my colleagues in the *Press* the next day, their reactions were mixed. John J. Dunne warned me that the Abbey would string me along and then dump me. 'Get something from them in writing,' he said. Adrian was more encouraging. He was the eternal optimist. 'You're in the door,' he said. 'They'll do it.'

I spent another eight months rewriting the script along the lines suggested by McCarthy. I was once more back in the admission ward of St Patrick's, a patient again in spirit. I wandered the ward and eavesdropped on strange conversations, observed all the minute details of the patients' behaviour. I consulted Pop again on the mood and colours of Dublin during the war years. He watched me with a mixture of pride and desperate hope. He must have asked himself many times would I see this through, or would I abandon it all for the bottle. I knew that a prayer often trembled about his lips during those long evenings in the winter of 1982.

But a play in the Abbey was too great a prize to throw away for the temporary pleasures of alcohol. The redrafting helped keep me sober. As the weeks wore on, I became increasingly obsessive about the play. I was going mad again, clicking away on the typewriter into the small hours. When I went to an AA meeting, they warned me about the play. I was tripping out again, they said, on a new addiction. I knew they were right, but I was powerless, as fear of failure drove me on relentlessly. So too did the compulsion to salvage something from the wreckage of my life.

Pop turned out to be a great source of information about the variety theatres of Dublin. He and my mother had often gone to the Theatre Royal on Sunday nights. He knew both Martin and Paddy Crosbie, who were well-known variety artists.

He also knew about Freddy Doyle. My aunts adored this matinée idol. He might have been as camp as a Christmas cracker, but they would never have understood what homosexuality was.

The Houlihan family, who lived next door, also had connections with the Royal, and Jimmy Campbell, who conducted the orchestra there, often played cards with the

Houlihan sisters. These sisters inhabited a completely different universe to that of my aunts. They drank gin and dated men with flashy cars. I remember musical evenings from my childhood with the piano playing next door and trained voices belting out Edwardian-era tunes. All this went into *The Midnight Door*.

Two weeks after I handed in the finished draft of the play, Sean McCarthy rang me with the news that the Abbey had decided to give it a rehearsed reading. It felt like a kick in the stomach.

'What did I tell you,' John J. Dunne said the next day. 'That shower are notorious for mucking people around.' But a rehearsed reading seemed closer to a full production. '*Festina lente*' kept coming into my thoughts. So too did the man in the Meath Hospital who had spent an entire day lifting a naggin of whiskey up the side of his bed. And McCarthy had reassured me that this was simply another step in the production process.

The reading was held in the rehearsal room on the top floor of the Abbey Theatre. There was an invited audience of theatre people. I particularly liked Eileen Colgan's Maggie: she made the character burst forth. I thought that the reading went very well. People laughed at the right times and there was genuine stillness for moments of pathos. But afterwards, Sean McCarthy came over to me and I knew by his apologetic expression that the news was not good. He said that the Abbey's artistic director, Joe Dowling, felt that the play 'was not there yet'. It would require another rewrite. For a moment, I believed that John J. Dunne might have been right after all. But McCarthy's belief in the play prevented me from succumbing to such doubts. 'It's almost there,' he kept saying. 'Just concentrate on building up tension in the scenes.' I knew what he meant. The reading flowed seamlessly, but it lacked dramatic impetus. I had sensed that myself during the reading, but I had desperately hoped that I was wrong.

So for the next couple of months, I worked on another draft. I rewrote every scene so that the drama moved towards a climax. The play took over my life. I could not sleep. I worked feverishly every night into the small hours. I bored my colleagues in the *Press* with my constant talk about it. Graham Sennett, the theatre columnist on the *Evening Press*, advised me to put it away for a few months – that I was too close to it and was in danger of losing the plot. John J. Dunne said that I should give it to another company. 'Do you know nothing about that crowd?' he raged at me one morning. I sensed that he was talking from his own experience. 'They'll string you along until there is a change of management, and then your play will be rejected by the new artistic director.'

But I trusted Sean McCarthy. He was a man of immense integrity. I decided to finish this new draft, and if the Abbey was still not satisfied, I would give it to the Gate, which had already expressed an interest in it.

When I had completed the new draft, I sent it to McCarthy and waited. I came very close to drink during that waiting period. My nerves were stretched to breaking point. I'm certain that Pop found the tension in the house unendurable as I smoked ceaselessly through the sleepless nights, or snapped at him constantly. The smell of alcohol wafting from the pubs of Burgh Quay tormented me. I went to AA meetings in search of peace, but found only confusion and torment. I desperately wanted to be drunk again, and adrift in some miasma of forgetfulness.

Then, after two weeks, Sean McCarthy rang me with the news I craved. The Abbey had formally accepted the play for a full production in the Peacock the following April. I had done it at last. Now I really did deserve a drink.

I sneaked into a pub in Talbot Street and drank myself into a delighted stupor, the alcohol releasing all the tension of the previous few months. A group of students sat near me and I told them about my play. They probably thought that I was some hallucinating drunk, but they celebrated with me all the same. I poured vodka down my throat as if I had come stumbling out of the desert, parched and delirious.

A familiar face loomed out of the fog. It was Harold, the sex maniac from Ward 3B. He eyed me suspiciously and sat down beside me. 'I sneaked out when the visitors were leaving,' he said, panting. He seemed sane now, and the predatory look had gone from his eyes.

'How will you get back?' I asked him.

He laughed. 'I'll worry about that when I'm good and drunk.'

I hadn't realised that Harold was also an alcoholic, and one of the club. I had thought that he was just mad. But here, drinking in the noisy pub, he was transformed, as he delighted in telling me some outlandish stories about his drinking escapades. Harold was normal after all. He told me that he was a retired history teacher and that his ambition was to go on one last, gigantic bender. He had been dried out more than a hundred times in virtually every psychiatric hospital in the country, and he was obviously proud of that achievement. 'I'm on the *Titanic*, son, steaming into hell. It's great,' he chortled, and raised his glass. He had been in and out of St Patrick's three times since I had left.

His present incarceration had come about after the police found him flashing late one night outside the convent where he had taught. 'I knew that fucking Mother Superior was watching me from her window, so I gave the old battleaxe a going-away present.' The police brought him to Grangegorman, but somehow Harold managed to get transferred to St Patrick's. He was still so befuddled that he didn't know if he was facing charges of indecent exposure. But he wasn't worried – not there in the company of drunks and lunatics. 'Even if I do get a spell in jail, it will be worth it, just for the pleasure of seeing that witch's outraged face,' he said with boyish glee. I gathered that he had spent years of drudgery teaching in the convent – years that had been occasionally enlivened by the prospect of escape into anarchy.

When closing time came, Harold was too helpless to move. 'Time to be getting back, Harold,' a barman said. 'I've rung you a taxi.' It was obvious that Harold escaped from the hospital quite frequently and this barman was in on the secret.

I shared the taxi with him. 'I usually tell them I was out at some AA meeting,' he said, with a mischievous wink, as he struggled to extract his huge frame from the taxi when we reached the hospital. The taxi then brought me up Infirmary Road to home. I prayed that Pop was in bed asleep. But when I stumbled into the hallway, he was there, waiting for me. The look of pain in his eyes haunts me to this day. He said nothing, and went into his room.

I stayed in bed for the next two days to dry out. Pop carried on as normal. I heard him downstairs, searching presses and drawers in case I had hidden a bottle of vodka somewhere. What should have been a happy celebration of having a play accepted by the Abbey had turned into a shattering disappointment. I cursed my wretched weakness as I sweated the sickly, sweet-smelling poison out of my system. My body trembled from head to toe as the sleepless hours dragged on interminably.

On the second night, just as the sweats began, I saw tiny, beetle-like creatures crawl out of an imaginary hole in the bedroom wall. I tried to close my eyes, but the furiously scuttling swarm compelled me to watch. Soon the bedroom wall was alive with these hideous insects. They swarmed across the floor and up onto the bed. Some took wing and buzzed around the room. I threw off the duvet in a panic. The light came on. Pop was at the bedroom door. I must have woken him up with my terrified screams. He had a glass of water in his hand. 'Take these,' he said calmly as he handed me some capsules of Librium. 'I kept them, just in case.'

He sat on the bed and stayed with me until the sedatives began to work and the plague of insects vanished back into the roseate patterns of the wallpaper. I could feel his warm hand on my forehead. He was whispering a prayer, imploring his god to banish these winged demons from my mind. I drifted into sleep.

Next morning, when I went downstairs, drained and shaky, Pop calmly said: 'Now you know what it does to you.' I promised him that I would never drink again. I'm sure he wanted to believe me, but how could he? I didn't even believe it myself.

13

Rehearsals started on a wet Monday morning in March 1983. I went along early and waited outside St George's Church in Hardwicke Street, where the rehearsals were to be held. An elderly woman, laden down with plastic shopping bags, was sheltering in a nearby doorway. It was Marie Kean, then Ireland's leading actress; I had seen her in numerous plays and films. She was to play Maggie – and not Eileen Colgan, who had had her heart set on the role. When I introduced myself to Marie, she immediately launched into a tirade about the terrible bus service from Rush, where she lived. 'I'm half the morning getting here,' she complained.

Once we were inside the cavernous rehearsal space, the director, Ben Barnes, introduced me to the rest of the cast: Ray MacAnally, David Kelly, Des Cave, Maureen Toal, Eamon Hunt and Nick Grennell. The first reading was dominated by MacAnally's overwhelming personality. He immediately let it be known that he was an authority on alcoholism. I noticed Marie Kean grimacing. They apparently didn't like each other much, and the tension between them became obvious later on when Ms Keane would excuse herself and leave the room whenever Ray had a big scene. Ray never stopped explaining the mysterious processes of acting: he made it sound as complicated as cosmic physics. But I never found him boring, and I often sensed that he was quite a lonely man despite his stature as the country's leading actor.

On one occasion, he began changing the script, and I objected. Maureen Toal whispered in my ear: 'Don't cross him, for heaven's sake, or he'll have another fucking heart attack.' But MacAnally was magnanimous, and gracefully conceded after a short discussion about the problematic lines of dialogue.

David Kelly played Fred (or Gerty, as I now called the character), and he was delightful: dapper, good-humoured, with a treasury of funny theatrical stories which he entertained us with every day. He was Fred incarnate, and as he played off MacAnally's Mr B., I could see that the pairing of these actors was an inspired piece of casting. They brought their own insights and experiences to the characters, so that after a short time, I felt I was back once more in the company of Fred and Mr B.

Midway through rehearsals, I got a phone call late one night from Marie Kean. She said that she couldn't take direction from Ben Barnes any more and would be leaving the show the next day. Ben was then a very young director and was obviously nervous of the prickly Ms Kean. When I mentioned this to Maureen Toal, she advised me to ignore it. Maureen was wise to all the ego displays and petty personal politics of the rehearsal room. Marie Kean never mentioned the phone call again, and she went on to deliver a great performance, one of prim grandeur and tightly controlled emotion. It was not the blowsy, wounded soubrette that I had envisioned, but it was still a powerful and truthful interpretation of the character.

'We'll have to make it work,' MacAnally said several times. This unsettled me. In my naivety, I thought: why couldn't he just play the part as it is written? But Ray had to get right under the skin of the character. Watching him work was like observing a magician conjuring up magic from the unlikeliest sources. I warmed to him more and more as the rehearsals went on. We often went for coffee afterwards, and we would talk about the problems that were besetting the *Press*. I had heard that he was a difficult man to work with, but that was not my experience. There seemed to be considerable depths of pain and honesty in the man. This was borne out by the performance he eventually delivered. He was Mr B. completely: a broken man, on the edge of permanent madness. Des Cave played the part of an English writer of children's stories who is haunted by a paedophile crime. His performance was eerily brilliant. He had that hunted look of a man besieged by demons and terrible memories.

At the first dress rehearsal in the Peacock, I was quite startled when Maureen Toal came onstage as the nurse. The costume department had dressed her as a French nun, with an enormous raised veil which made her look like Mother Mary Aikenhead. It was my first inkling of the dangers inherent in the Abbey, where stage brilliance was sometimes compromised by sheer idiocy. There was a rapid change of costume, and the dress rehearsal continued. I was happy with Ben Barnes' production, as it captured the atmosphere of a psychiatric hospital very well. Kelly and MacAnally shifted from the hilarious to the pathetic with perfect timing, and they brought a note of tragedy to the lives of Fred and Mr B.

The opening night was a terrifying experience. I felt completely exposed. I knew most of the newspaper people in the audience. I also knew the depths of their cynicism, for I too had plumbed those depths when I was a wearied, self-regarding theatre critic. Now, I was plagued by fear and paranoia, and as the lights went down, I sank into my seat, almost afraid to watch the stage. Des Rush from the *Irish Independent* sat beside me. Fifteen minutes into the play, he nudged me and said: 'This is terrific.' I relaxed a little. But despite the congratulations afterwards, I was still uneasy. I knew, from my years as a journalist, not to trust the backslapping theatrics of an opening night. I also felt that everything had been too easy, from the Abbey accepting my play to them giving me their finest performers. There had to be a catch somewhere. As I mingled nervously with the luvvies and the newspaper hacks in the Peacock bar, I was convinced that the gods had some salutary lesson in store. Pop, however, glowed with pride. The aunts seemed torn between pride and embarrassment. I knew that they were uneasy about my parading my experiences of alcoholism in such a public fashion. My brothers and sisters were just relieved that I was sober.

My uneasiness was reinforced the next morning when I went out at first light to get the papers. I read the *Irish Times* review first. It said: '*The Midnight Door* is not just a failure, it is a depressing failure.' That cut deep – right to the core of all my insecurities. Although Des Rush of the *Independent* and Con Houlihan of the *Press* both described the play as 'a triumph', and all the other critics echoed these sentiments, the wound inflicted by the *Times* critic was to fester for years afterwards.

The reactions of Joe Dowling and Ben Barnes to the *Times* review gave me another insight into the mindset of the Abbey Company. Though every other newspaper and magazine hailed the play and the production, the Abbey's main concern was the negative review in the *Times*. The opinions of Houlihan, O'Toole and Hosey seemed to be of less importance to them than those of a second-string critic from the *Irish Times*.

Adrian McLoughlin was not surprised. 'That shower in the Abbey take their cue from the *Irish Times* arts pages. Nobody else matters.'

John J. Dunne joined in the post-mortem. 'Nothing,' he said, hissing with rage, 'nothing demonstrates the parochialism of this banana republic better than the link between the crowd of pseudos in the *Times* and the shower of gobshites in Abbey Street. They go together like bacon and cabbage.' My *Press* colleagues took the *Times* review personally.

The play packed out for most nights of its three-week run. The Sunday papers and the radio reviews were all glowing, and I was delighted that the *Times* published the only bad review of the eighteen notices which the play received. Pop came with me on most nights, for he too had become an integral part of the play's creation. He became very friendly with Marie Kean.

One Wednesday night towards the end of the run, Ben Barnes met me in the foyer and said very crossly: 'The house is only half-full.' Somehow that was my fault. Then, after the last performance, we had a party in the Abbey bar. I overheard someone ask Marie Kean what the reviews were like. 'Ah, mixed,' she said sourly. 'There's nothing "mixed" about one bad review in eighteen,' I said to her angrily, but she smiled grimly and inscrutably into her drink.

The *Times* review seemed to have poisoned the air in the Abbey. I found the naivety of the Abbey management baffling. Did they seriously believe that all critics were motivated by the best intentions? I had seen critics stumble into the *Press*, slobbering with rage – and drink – as they set about dissecting a play or film. I had done it myself when I was befuddled by drink – groping through a jungle of clichés for the most scabrous put-down.

When *The Midnight Door* ended, I started writing another play, *The Dosshouse Waltz*. This was also about people living on the margins of Irish society. I entered it for the O. Z. Whitehead play competition and it won first prize. I then gave it to Phyllis Ryan for the Dublin Theatre Festival. She was one of Ireland's best producers, and though she did not have the resources of the Abbey, she could still conjure riches from a depleted chest. My career as a playwright was taking off. I was starting to enjoy the freedom of sobriety for the first time since my teenage years.

The Dosshouse Waltz was about a group of winos living in a derelict Georgian building in Dublin. Seamus Forde and Brendan Cauldwell played former barristers who drifted into the streets as a result of alcoholism and madness. They teamed up with Anna Manahan, as Sadie, a character who was also from a respectable background, and Donal O'Kelly, who played a young heroin addict called Hopkins. In a frantic effort to crawl his way back to respectability, the Cauldwell character persuades Sadie to whore for him. The play is a dark Dublin take on the Pygmalion theme.

We had great fun with one particular scene in which Sadie returns with a fish which she got from a client. I based the scene on a strange episode in my past.

When I was a teenager and still at school, I joined the Legion of Mary. We used to do what was called 'street contact' work, which meant stopping people in the street and asking them about their religion. One night, I was with a senior member of the Legion in Grafton Street when we stopped a big, broad-shouldered man, aged about thirty. He had a strong Dublin accent and worked on the docks. He said that he did some 'work on the side' which would make him an unsuitable candidate for the Legion of Mary. Every Friday night, he said, he went down to the fish market and bought a large, oily mackerel. He then went to a basement apartment in Fitzwilliam Square, where a middle-aged businessman lay in wait for him, his naked body spread-eagled across an ironing board. 'I just beat his arse with the mackerel, and that made him happy. It was worth the few bob anyways,' the docker said. 'Then I'd bring the fish home and the wife cooked it for dinner. It always tasted nice, as well.'

The scene, as played out by Anna Manahan, a prudishly outraged Seamus Forde and a drunken Brendan Cauldwell, was quite hilarious, as the actors tossed the slippery fish about the stage. 'I'm not eating that thing after where it has been!' roared Seamus. A fresh fish had to be bought every night for the scene.

The fact that my plays were about low life never seemed to bother Pop. In fact, he liked the humanity of the characters and recognised many of them from my conversations about the *Press* and the pub life around Burgh Quay. His favourite play of mine was *Private Death of a Queen*, which Phyllis Ryan staged in the Eblana for the 1986 Dublin Theatre Festival. This was a play about old age, and the loss of independence and dignity that came with it. Pop was central to the writing of this: I often talked to him about his fears of old age. Once, when I asked him what his biggest fear was, he said 'going into a nursing home'.

The origins of the play lay in the variety show which Fred staged in St Patrick's Hospital. I remember thinking that a play, written and produced by patients in an institution, would be a useful device for exploring the realities of old age and approaching death. I thought it would deliver a greater dramatic punch if I made it a black comedy. In *Private Death of a Queen*, the characters in an old folks' home stage their own play about the death of Queen Elizabeth I. Anna Manahan brilliantly played Nonie, a character who realises that she has been abandoned in the home by her family. This realisation deepens her portrayal of the dying, loveless queen. The play-within-a-play is an anarchic account of Elizabeth's last days, but it is also a metaphor for the insecurities and disappointments of old age.

The play received mixed notices. The *Irish Times* was very positive for a change. The critic on the *Evening Press* took offence at the unruly behaviour of the characters and made the ridiculous claim that 'old folks don't engage in or talk about sex'.

During one performance, I noticed a couple sitting in front of me. They sat stiff and po-faced throughout the play. I was furious, and wanted to bang their heads together and say: 'Laugh, for Christ's sake.' When the show was over, the gentleman turned to his partner and said, wearily: 'Well, that never got off the ground.' Such reactions still provoked homicidal instincts in me. The critic-turned-playwright was desperate for acclamation.

14

By the summer of 1988, I had had five plays staged, three for the Abbey and two for Phyllis Ryan's Gemini company. Yet, with every play came the old doubts and fears. Where was the hidden trap in all this apparent success? In my confused state back then, I often wondered where the real source of my madness lay. Was it in alcoholism or in something deeper? The characters in my head were broken inmates screaming for release, and I found it impossible to put emotional distance between myself and them. The theatre was the obvious terminus for my troubled journey through a black 1960s childhood, the *Press* and the mental institution. The theatre, with its illusions and heightened emotions, its shadows and echoes, its yearnings and make-believe, was my natural home. I stumbled towards it like a pilgrim, plagued by demons and craving salvation.

In May, a new play called *Sea Urchins* opened in the Hawkswell Theatre in Sligo, and it was very well received. It was based on a 'queer-bashing' murder which had been committed in Fairview Park, Dublin, in 1982. The play explored three subjects about which I had very strong views: homophobia, homelessness and addiction. The young company which staged it, Acorn, were fired with energy and passion, and working with them was probably the most satisfying experience I had as a playwright. The actual murderer in the play, Huey, is a repressed homosexual, full of self-disgust and rage. In the murder scene, we witness him viciously kicking his victim to death, but we know that he is really destroying something deep within himself. We developed the play in a rehearsal room in Sligo. This workshop process gave the play an urgency which translated onto the stage.

I wanted to write about the Fairview Park case from the point of view of the killers themselves. This enabled me to explore the warped psychology that feeds homophobia. In the 1980s, homosexuality was still taboo in Ireland. The perpetrators of the Fairview Park crime were convicted of manslaughter but were treated leniently by the courts. Their defence was that they believed that their victim was a homosexual. They were given suspended sentences and they walked free from the court, to join a noisy crowd of supporters who paraded through Fairview shouting 'Queers out!' One of the gang was convicted less than a year later of raping a pregnant American visitor.

Not long after the Fairview Park case, another homosexual, Charles Self, was found murdered in Dublin city centre. Self was a producer in RTÉ. The police investigating the crime did a trawl of all gay people in Dublin. They visited offices and homes, telling wives that their husbands were gay and warning employers about 'the queers' in their midst. They also fingerprinted hundreds of frightened gay men. They made it clear that all gay men in Dublin were suspects. They never found the murderer of Charles Self.

This sinister census of Dublin's gay community made a mockery of the Irish government's contention that while homosexual acts were criminal in the Irish Republic, the laws were never enforced. It was to be another decade before these Victorian laws were repealed – a decade in which some public figures came out of the closet but many gay people, especially in rural and working-class areas, continued to live in fear.

The tabloids, especially, were virulently anti-gay even as late as the 1980s. When a young Fine Gael councillor was arrested and charged with soliciting on Burgh Quay, his photograph was splashed across the front pages under lurid headlines describing him as a 'pervert'. The 'queer-bashers' got plenty of encouragement from Church and State.

After *Sea Urchins* opened in the Project, Pop took off to the country for a holiday. He turned eighty-one that June. I offered to go with him but he joked that if Ronald Reagan could run America, then he was quite capable of going off on a train journey on his own to Tipperary. He often took risks to demonstrate that he still possessed the strength of a young man. I returned home from the *Press* one day in January to find him out on the roof of our four-storey house, shovelling away the snow. It seemed cruel to tell him that he was too old for such tasks. He went to Tipperary to visit my mother's relations, whom he hadn't seen in many years – not since her death. It did not seem strange to me that he had decided on a whim to go. He just said 'I haven't been down to Tipperary in ages', and then embarked upon his peculiar ritual of preparation, which I had grown so used to over the years. He washed all his old socks, shirts and underwear, and for a week the clothesline resembled a set for *Robinson Crusoe*. Then he packed everything into his ancient suitcase and set off for Heuston Station, a boyish gleam of adventure in his eyes.

While he was away, I decided to go back to visit St Patrick's Hospital. I had avoided going there for years, though Fred and Mr B. were always in my head – two raging queens who refused to be forgotten. So one afternoon, while coming home from the *Press*, I found myself turning left from the Quays and up the familiar hill of St Stephen's Lane. When I got to the gates of the hospital, my instinct was to run away. This was the past, I told myself. But the hospital looked different. It had been completely refurbished and now had a bright new red-brick entrance. The gloomy eighteenth-century building which had once imprisoned me was gone, vanished behind a façade of glass and potted plants. Now the place looked like a suburban garden centre. I walked in. There was nothing familiar there any more – apart from Bridie Butt, who was busily working the large entrance lounge. Even the canteen looked different. The patients seemed younger and more normal than before, and there was no sign of those Largactyl-driven ghosts who had haunted this place years earlier.

I followed the signs out to the back of the hospital, where the geriatric ward was discreetly hidden away behind a fuchsia-hedged tennis court. Fred was sitting in the bay window of the day room with a blanket covering his legs. He looked like a pantomime dame, caked in make-up and with purple dye in his hair. I sat in the seat next to him. He didn't seem to recognise me. 'Is the tea up yet?' he asked, without taking his eyes off the blanket. When I inquired about Mr B., he blinked in incomprehension.

The August sun flooded this chamber, casting cruel light on everything. Most of the patients sat listlessly in their armchairs, gaping at the television set in the corner. A nurse kept watch from another corner of the room, her radio blaring beside her. Freddie Mercury's strangulated screams drowned out any sound from the television, and seemed hideously appropriate in this setting. An enormously fat woman waddled over to us, and stood in front of Fred. Then she started to tug at his blanket. Fred whimpered 'I always sit here', but the woman continued to pull. There was no expression on her face. I offered her my seat, but she ignored me and continued harrying poor Fred. Eventually, the nurse came over and said 'Come on, Betty, be a good girl now', and led the fat woman to another armchair. I offered Fred a cigarette. He examined it and then put it in his dressing-gown pocket. A moment later, he decided to smoke it. We sat in silence for nearly an hour, but when I was getting up to leave, he turned to look at me. There was no sign at all of Fred in those distant eyes. On the way out, a nurse told me that Mr B. had died in Grangegorman about a year before. 'You got Fred on a bad day,' she said.

Adrian McLoughlin went back on the drink that summer. He had been in hospital earlier in the year for a 'stomach complaint' – his euphemism – and that brush with death had undermined him completely. I went to see him in the Mater Hospital. He was obsessed with the details of his ailment, talking incessantly about colostomies without a trace of irony or fear. But not long after his discharge from hospital, he was back drinking with grim determination in the pubs around Burgh Quay.

There was a great deal of excitement in those pubs now, as the last scenes of the *Press* drama began to unfold. An American investor came on board, promising salvation. The *Irish Press* was relaunched as a tabloid, and everybody felt that the years of uncertainty were over. Strange-looking Americans came into the newsroom every day to run the paper. They explained that the newspaper market was now dominated by youth. As a consequence of this discovery, the *Irish Press* began to look like a brash and lurid comic, peppered with trivia about television celebrities. The newsroom was suddenly full of breezy teenage reporters. John J. Dunne took early retirement, and went to write more ghost stories in his shabby bachelor's house in Santry. Theo's services were no longer required, and he was packed off to drink his last years away in a room in Blessington Street. Adrian was put in charge of the television pages. This was regarded as a promotion, but Adrian was aggrieved. He had been moved sideways, he felt, because he was sick; and sick, middle-aged men were a liability.

The American chief executive was a long stick insect of a man who wore a polka-dot bow tie. He had a Swedish name and came from Salt Lake City. He and his minions seemed like CIA agents – a race of dull, ungainly giants, who looked ludicrously out of place in Burgh Quay. They held meetings every day at which earnest young Wilburs and Harry Juniors sat around with their legs coiled about their armpits, endlessly discussing marketing strategies.

But before long, the euphoria turned sour. The marketing experts discovered that the traditional republican readership of the *Press* had vanished, and the fabulous youth market had failed to materialise.

I had been sober now for many years. I still went to AA meetings, but more out of habit than desire. I never found real sanctuary in those rooms. Well-heeled, reformed drunks spoke in evangelical terms about their deliverance: 'I can now smell the grass growing every day' or 'I know who I am at last'. These sentiments left me cold. After one meeting in a school in Donnybrook, I met the woman who had spoken to us in the hospital years earlier. When I confided in her that AA wasn't working for me, she displayed one of those insufferable grins of the righteous and said that I would drink again. She had absolutely no doubt about that.

When Pop came back from his travels through Tipperary, I noticed a big change in him. He had become quieter, more withdrawn. On some mornings he came down for breakfast looking tired and frail. 'There's nothing the matter with me,' he said unconvincingly, but I could see that he was getting slower and stiffer, and was now a little gloomy. I wondered was it the emotional stress of returning to Mother's home, meeting my uncles and cousins, and reliving so many happier times, when they had both gone to Tipperary every September for the harvest? His sudden quietness created an eerily unsettling mood in the house. I could hear him moving about late at night, going in and out of rooms. Occasionally, a cough or a deep melancholy sigh would break the silence. Common sense told me that he was dying, but I refused to believe the obvious little signs. I told myself that this would pass. He would come out of his room one morning, and that shy, boyish gleam would be back in his eyes.

Bridie Houlihan came in from next door to join him for breakfast. She was the last of her family, and she drank gin in the evenings to compensate for her loneliness. She brought Pop the *Irish Independent,* which he never read. Bridie would announce herself in the hallway with a wheezy 'Yoo hoo!' and then bustle into the kitchen for her ritual cup of tea and two cigarettes. She often seemed surprised to see Pop still presiding over his breakfast in the dark kitchen. Bridie would relax into some garbled account of the previous night's television. Since the other members of her family had died, she had become more and more reliant on the television. She talked about the characters in *Coronation Street* as if they were special friends. They, and her glass of gin, were her sole companions in the long evenings of her twilight.

She said to Pop in her usual brusque manner: 'You all right, Jim?' He said that he was feeling a bit tired and might see a doctor.

'What would you want to see a doctor for?' she barked. Then she pulled furiously on her cigarette. 'Leave well enough alone,' she gasped.

She was eighty-four and he was eighty-one. They had both struggled this far under their respective loads of sorrow, without benefit of doctors or medicines. Every day now was a small triumph. Pop nodded in agreement. Leaving well enough alone had always been his philosophy.

When she had finished her tea, she would wash her cup under the cold tap, and then flutter off to attend to the multitude of mundane tasks which made up her day.

As Pop declined, I began to realise how important his daily routines were. They provided the structure that kept him alive. He still insisted on walking the half-mile down to the supermarket, and then climbing back that steep ascent from Manor Street, his heart pounding and his legs weakening. It was a heroic act of will. He still cooked dinner, and afterwards, he washed and shaved for evening Mass. The only time he sat down to rest was in the evenings, when all his chores were done.

Sea Urchins opened in the Project Theatre, and I introduced Pop to the young cast. He had an encouraging word for each one of them. He felt that this was a duty he had to perform. The play turned out to be a great success and was booked out for the week's run. The reviews were also very encouraging. I remember Senator David Norris in particular lavishing such extravagant praise in his review on RTÉ that I had to stifle an impulse to go out and get drunk. Euphoria, I discovered, was as deadly as despair. Everyone connected to the production was on a high, but an old, uneasy feeling surfaced amid the celebrations. I detected Banquo's ghost at the edge of the party. Although Michael Finlan wrote a very positive review for the *Irish Times* when the play opened in Sligo, the paper decided to send another critic to review it again in Dublin. It was a repeat of his wretched *Midnight Door* performance. Alone among all the critics, he panned the play.

But the *Times* critic had no effect on the box office: *Sea Urchins* transferred to the Tivoli and ran, to full houses, for another eight weeks.

I was still not satisfied: the blow from the *Times* stirred up so much rage and paranoia, I found it almost impossible to resist drink. I contacted an alcoholism counsellor in St Patrick's Hospital and she helped me through the storm.

One night, towards the end of the run of *Sea Urchins*, an elderly American couple stood up during the play and shouted abuse at the cast. 'This play is anti-Semitic! It is a disgrace!' they screamed, as the manager tried to usher them out of the theatre. 'Whoever wrote this filth should be burned!' the old woman raged. I couldn't fathom how they managed to conclude that the play was anti-Semitic. They may have misinterpreted a line in the play which refers to the murdered homosexual as 'a dirty old jeweller'. The protest was widely covered in the newspapers the next day and the publicity helped the play enormously.

As August drifted into autumn, Pop's darkness deepened. He now started to get up later and later in the day, sometimes as late as noon, and struggled down the stairs to the kitchen. Once, I noticed him staring at the wall. He had sat down to catch his breath after the struggle down the stairs, and for a moment he was mesmerised by the blank kitchen wall. I was shocked to see how much his face had changed. It had just caved in around his eyes. I pleaded with him to see a doctor. 'For what?' he replied with a wintry smile. Another morning, I saw him climbing out of the bath. His body had shrunk so much that for a second I didn't recognise him. That footballer's physique, glowing in those family photographs upstairs, had now been plundered by old age. As surely as Fred and Mr B. had faded into the chaos of St Patrick's Hospital, Pop was vanishing before my eyes. He spent more time in his room tidying things away, folding up letters and cards and stashing them away in boxes in the wardrobe.

In September, he collapsed in the church during evening Mass. He didn't want to go in the ambulance. He said that he would be fine once he got home to bed. But the ambulance men persuaded Pop to accompany them 'just in case'. This was not supposed to happen – not yet, not before I had rebuilt my life and put all the ghosts that were between us finally to rest. I needed a few more years with him, a few months, even weeks, to show him that I was cured and ready now to deal straight with him. I needed to tell him, even if he didn't want to hear, the full truth about my breakdown. I needed to clear the air, so that our relationship could be grounded in truth and not in denial. But once I heard that the ambulance had brought him to hospital and that he had put up a terrible struggle to get home again, I knew that the game was up for both of us.

I got a phone call in the Tivoli Theatre. When I got to the Mater Hospital, he was in the casualty ward, stranded on a stretcher amid drunks and quarrelsome drug addicts. I thought he looked OK, if a little flushed in the face. He asked me to take him home. I knew that he had had these turns before. He just went to bed and was all right the next morning. He pleaded with me to take him home, but the doctor insisted that he stay overnight, 'just in case'. Just in case of what? I wondered. But I was really too upset to protest. So they wheeled him up to the ward. He looked like a frightened baby.

The next morning, I could see that he had deteriorated. His breathing was laboured. He looked miserable, trapped in a bed that was too small for him. His face was thinner and greyer. There were tubes sticking out of every part of him. He was worried about not being able to go to the toilet. I told him that there was urine in one of the tubes that ran from his body down the side of the bed. I was lying, but I needed to reassure him. He couldn't face it. *I* couldn't face it. Death is so ugly that we desperately need to conceal its overtures with half-truths and evasions, with denials. One by one, my brothers and sisters appeared. There was panic in their eyes. We sat around Pop's bed, watching and waiting.

Then he seemed to vanish from life. One minute we were chatting away to him, and then he was gone. There was no struggle or pain. In mid-sentence, he just faded into eternity, a wisp of a smile on his shrunken face. I stared at him for ages, not knowing what to do. I wanted to reach into the black void and pull him back out again. I saw his smile fade and his eyes fall away, and I heard myself gasp as my sister screamed for a nurse.

'Don't forget to pay the gas bill.' Those were his last words.

Maybe it was for the best that I didn't open up to him in the hospital. What could I have said to him anyway? Where could I have begun? Would the words 'I'm sorry, Pop' have been enough? If I had told him about my homosexuality, would it have freed me from shame? I doubt it. It was to take many more years, and numerous relapses into alcoholism, before I could accept it myself – and that acceptance came only after I was exhausted by the struggle of living a lie.

He was more concerned in those last few hours with the discomfort of his ward bed and the frightening implications of all the tubes sticking into his body. Why would I have burdened him with cruel honesty? I had to let it go.

He was always a shy man, but he did express his feelings, often in a bizarre and humorous way. Here was a man who had buried a young wife and had had to endure a son's madness. Yet he coped. Unlike all the wounded, disappointed losers in my plays, in the *Press* and in the hospital, he was a winner. His quiet, humdrum life was a small triumph.

I can still see him, seven foot tall in my old, discarded platform boots, coming up the road from evening Mass. His head may have been full of grief, yet his laughter was ironic and compassionate. He towered over the neatly trimmed hedges of his contemporaries, hidden away behind their lace curtains. What did they think, these ancient neighbours, when they saw him pass by like a giant? That he was mad? That grief had finally struck him down? I suspect that they sensed a young spirit that refused to be cowed by time. 'There goes Jim, and it's younger he's getting every day.'

I whispered to him on his deathbed that I would remain sober for the rest of my days. This time I believed it. I hoped, with remorse tearing my insides apart, that he heard me. Maybe he did know my secrets, after all. Maybe he knew and, like me, found comfort in denial. One cannot really hide from a parent. I know that now.

Death clarified so much in an instant.

The next morning, the Abbey rang to say that rehearsals for my new play, *Josephine in the Night*, were to start the following week. It was a one-woman show, with Maureen Toal playing the Empress Josephine in her last days in the gloomy splendour of Malmaison near Paris. But in the confusion and grief of Pop's illness and death, I had forgotten about the play. At his funeral, the Empress Josephine was nowhere in my thoughts. Nor was the Abbey, or the critics, or the doomed *Irish Press*. It was just Pop and my mother, united again – at least in my imagination.